The IMMIGRANT in AMERICAN HISTORY

harper ⚜ torchbooks

EDITORS' NOTE: *A check-list of Harper Torchbooks, classified by subjects, is printed at the end of this volume.*

The IMMIGRANT in AMERICAN HISTORY

BY
MARCUS LEE HANSEN

Edited with a Foreword by
ARTHUR M. SCHLESINGER

HARPER TORCHBOOKS
THE CLOISTER LIBRARY

HARPER & ROW, PUBLISHERS
NEW YORK, EVANSTON, AND LONDON

THE IMMIGRANT IN AMERICAN HISTORY

Copyright, 1940
by the President and Fellows of Harvard College

Printed in the United States of America.

This book was originally published in 1940 by
Harvard University Press and is here reprinted
by arrangement.

First HARPER TORCHBOOK edition published 1964 by
Harper & Row, Publishers, Incorporated
49 East 33rd Street
New York 16, N.Y.

These States are the amplest poem,
Here is not merely a nation, but a teeming nation of nations.

> WALT WHITMAN, *Chants Democratic and
> Native American*

CONTENTS

	EDITOR'S FOREWORD	ix
I.	MIGRATIONS OLD AND NEW	3
II.	THE ODYSSEY OF THE EMIGRANT	30
III.	IMMIGRATION AND EXPANSION	53
IV.	IMMIGRATION AND DEMOCRACY	77
V.	IMMIGRATION AND PURITANISM	97
VI.	IMMIGRATION AND AMERICAN CULTURE	129
VII.	THE SECOND COLONIZATION OF NEW ENGLAND	154
VIII.	MIGRATION ACROSS THE NORTHERN BORDER	175
IX.	IMMIGRATION AS A FIELD FOR HISTORICAL RESEARCH	191
	INDEX	219

EDITOR'S FOREWORD

IN far too many instances the professionally trained historian never outgrows his tutelage. Though he is constantly discovering new facts about the past, he timidly continues to point out trees instead of describing forests. Skilled at taking pains, he forgets for what purpose alone it is worth taking pains. He neglects the broad view, the larger interrelationships, the deeper understanding, with the result that less capable hands are tempted to undertake the hazardous task of interpretation and generalization.

The author of these essays spent many years in both Europe and the United States investigating the history of immigration. In his two recent works, *The Atlantic Migration, 1607–1860* (Cambridge, 1940) and *The Mingling of the Canadian and American Peoples* (New Haven, 1940), he displayed his mastery of the historian's technique of intensively exploring specific aspects of the subject. But he regarded such inquiries as means to a more significant end: a better knowledge of the historical rôle of the immigrant in American life. For accomplishing this purpose Professor Hansen possessed unusual credentials. To his studies he brought not only assiduous research and a musing mind, but also the resources of personal and family experience arising from the fact that, as the son of foreign-born parents, he himself as a youth had observed the Americanizing process at work under

Midwestern conditions. He developed his larger views of immigration in lectures and articles. His untimely death in 1938 at the age of forty-five, while Professor of History at the University of Illinois, removed from the historical guild one whose services could ill be spared.

The importance of Professor Hansen's theme need not be argued in a country where nearly half of the white inhabitants are descended from postcolonial foreign stock. These later arrivals introduced differences of outlook and culture which greatly modified the basic Anglo-Saxon heritage and the whole pattern of American life. As a result, the old-stock American as well as the new found himself in the "melting pot," for he could not escape the influences of the social and intellectual environment which the more recent comers helped to fashion. The author's principal concern is with the nineteenth century. His method is telescopic rather than microscopic, though he never generalizes without reference to particulars. He sheds new light on obscure points and challenges accepted ideas. Many of his interpretations will doubtless serve as points of departure for detailed scholarly inquiries for the purpose of testing his views. No one knew better than he how tentative all judgments must be when the evidence is only partially known; and in the final paper of the volume he indicates the many nooks and crannies of the subject that still await investigation.

In editing the essays I have eliminated repetitive matter and made other minor changes and, in the case of those papers originally prepared as lectures, I have sought to remove the indications of informal oral delivery. The first four essays and the sixth are here published for the first time. The first, third, fourth, fifth and sixth formed part of a course of public lectures given at the University College, University of London, in February and March, 1935. "Immigration and Puritanism" appeared in the *Norwegian-American Studies*, IX (1936), 1–28. "The Second Colonization of New England" is reprinted from the *New England Quarterly*, II (1929), 539–560. "Migration across the Northern Border" was published originally under the title, "A Resumé of the History of Canadian-American Population Relations," in pages 95–106 of the *Proceedings* (Boston, 1937) of the Conference on Canadian-American Affairs held at Kingston, Ontario, on September 14–18, 1937. It summarizes the findings which Professor Hansen later elaborated in his book *The Mingling of the Canadian and American Peoples*. The concluding essay is adapted from an article which appeared under the title, "The History of American Immigration as a Field for Research," in the *American Historical Review*, XXXII (1926–1927), 500–518.

In discharging my editorial function I have been heartened by the interest shown by many of Professor Hansen's former students and by his professional colleagues in all parts of the country. More specifically, I am indebted to Mr. C. Frederick Hansen for helpful coöperation, to Dr. Henry G. H. Halvorson and Dr. Oscar Handlin for various favors, and to Miss Elizabeth F. Hoxie for putting the manuscript into shape for the press and preparing the index.

ARTHUR M. SCHLESINGER

The IMMIGRANT in AMERICAN HISTORY

I

MIGRATIONS OLD AND NEW

A SIGNIFICANT part of history deals with mankind in motion. The earliest legends tell of a hero fleeing before the wrath of the gods, of a chosen people wandering through the wilderness, of Italian tribes descending from the hills to found an imperial city on the plains. When the splendor of Rome disappears, it gives way to hordes of barbarians streaming through the passes of the Alps. The dim background of the Middle Ages is brightened by columns of knights riding eastward on the Crusades. In the fifteenth century three caravels sail bravely toward the rim of the world and a new era begins. Spanish conquerors, French adventurers, English seamen take possession of the western continent and in their wake come priests and soldiers, merchants and traders, Puritans and Cavaliers, Indian fighters and buffalo hunters — the red-blooded men whose exploits wrote the romance of colonial and pioneer days.

Less honored in song and story is another movement of mankind, which, if lacking in spectacular heroes, has nevertheless woven itself into the very warp and woof of American history. There was no glamour about the hardships of the steerage and, when the travelers disembarked on new shores, onlookers often saw in them nothing but stolid-faced, uncouth peasants who blindly followed the path of least resistance. But they were all human beings; they tore themselves loose from an environment which was life itself; they passed through strange lands; they tossed upon the sea; they served as drudges; and, finally, they were content if their children reaped the blessings that they had sought for themselves. In the century between 1815 and 1914 fifty million of these emigrants set out from Europe to all parts of the rising world. If an epic is the tale of a heroic soul struggling valiantly against hostile forces, then fifty million epics were lived between those years.

The statistician summarizes the history of the nineteenth century in a few pages. Columns of figures, graphs and charts reveal the changes out of which came politics and war. Industrial progress takes the form of so many tons of shipping, so many bars of pig iron, so many bushels of wheat, so many miles of railroads and cables. But to make the story complete, side by side with the tons, bars, bushels and miles must be placed the fifty million emigrants. They were a force of equal significance. Often it was their presence which made necessary the physical changes that statistics portray; usually it was their labor which brought the changes into being.

Among the factors that have shaped the last century it is easy to overlook these migrations. They flowed silently and smoothly with no governmental interference and little regulation. At the present time one never crosses an international boundary, with its formality of passports and visas, without overhearing an older traveler say to a younger, "It wasn't this way before the World War. You said you were an Englishman or an American, and that was all there was to it." To the traveler of 1800, however, such ceremonials would have seemed natural. He also was acquainted with the official certificate that revealed age, nationality and distinguishing marks. He also answered the questions: where from and whither bound; and on arrival he registered with the police and went about his business or pleasure, knowing that the watchful eye of authority was upon him.

But nineteenth-century liberalism did not relish restrictions upon the individual; and as its doctrines became embodied in official policies, the regulations were modified, and then repealed or allowed to fall into disuse. The world entered upon a period in which there was free trade in people, or, to use a more technical phrase, free trade in labor. Man power could be shifted to any quarter of the globe where hands or brains were needed to organize and develop the resources. This circumstance reflected the grand intercontinental specialization that prevailed before 1914. It represented a striving toward the ideal of the older economists that every continent and every island should concentrate upon those tasks for which Nature had endowed it. And so one European went to Australia and raised the wool that the mills of Lancashire manufactured into the clothing of the world. Another became a miner in South Africa, and the gold he dug provided the international medium of exchange. A third raised cattle in the Argentine, and his leather shod a million feet and belted the factory wheels of a dozen countries. A fourth produced grain on the American prairies, and his wheat fed all nations. Without migration, resources would have remained dormant awaiting a distant and uncertain time when the native populations would advance in numbers and skill to the point where they could capitalize on their soil, climate and geographic position.

To understand the importance of nineteenth-century migration, let us consider more specifically a few features characteristic of the age. One was the international competition in merchantmen to capture the trade of the seas. The history of every one of the great maritime transportation companies was intertwined with the history of emigration. Samuel Cunard, the Nova Scotian, received a subsidy for carrying the mails, but before long his principal business was the carrying of Irishmen to the New World. The White Star Line sent ships loaded with human cargoes over a network of routes that radiated from Glasgow, Liverpool and Belfast. German emigration transformed the decaying Hanseatic town of Bremen into a world port, and the North German Lloyd was organized to take care of this prosperous trade. Hamburg was aroused to action by the success of its rival and the Hamburg-American Line was the answer. The Italian Line appeared when the Mediterranean peoples began to swarm; and the French Line coöperated with the French railways to attract emigrants from Central Europe. Each of these companies built luxury liners, but the palm gardens and swimming pools did well if they paid for themselves. Profits were made and dividends were provided by the thousands of humble passengers crowded below, whose only desire was to reach the far side of the Atlantic.

A second aspect of nineteenth-century history was the internationalization of banking and finance which accompanied the commercial expansion. On the outward voyage European freighters carried locomotives and rails, pumps and drills for the mines, sometimes gold for the pay rolls. The economist describes this traffic as the export of capital and, when the statistician traces it upon his chart, he very properly finds a remarkable conformity to the fluctuations in the movement of European emigration. Without labor, capital was dead; without capital, labor was helpless. In the early decades of colonization they moved together. The trading company sent out goods and servants in the same vessel. In later times, although they proceeded by different ships and by different routes, ultimately they came together on the prairie or in the rising industrial town. The alliance was not always direct and usually not of long duration. The laborer appropriated for himself a part of the pioneer opportunities and, in turn, became a capitalist in need of labor. Thus the world was covered with a complex of credits, loans, interest payments and rates of exchange that have come to count so heavily in the life of each individual nation.

Observers whose patriotism took a practical turn bemoaned the departure of fellow citizens, saying, "We are losing our market." But often the loss was only temporary. It was impossible for the children of Israel to forget the fleshpots of Egypt; it was difficult for Europeans to forget the comforts and customs of their native lands. Every immigrant settlement became a purchaser of wares from home; and enterprising exporters used this beginning as an opening wedge for expanding their foreign trade. A new community demands more than an old; and, however unevenly it may have been divided among countries, Europe as a whole discovered an unexpected overseas market in the fifty million expatriates and their descendants. Unfortunately, this outlet was not permanent. In time, the settlers began to manufacture for themselves and the competition among the exporters became more acute. Hence it may be said that emigration was not without its effects upon the bitter trade rivalries that destroyed former international friendships and planted the seeds of war.

One other development of the century is important: the growth of imperialism. The British Empire which took shape in the nineteenth century differed essentially from what had gone before. It is not fantastic to believe that a clearer realization of the rôle of emigrants was one reason for the change. Was not the eventual concept of a Commonwealth of Nations a recognition of the existence of nations that had been created by groups of settlers? Not until the latter part of the century did Germany enter the field of colonial expansion; but Bismarck's efforts in Africa and the Far East had been preceded by a generation of agitation rooted in an anxious concern for the annual loss of blood and treasure represented by unending caravans of migrants. These dependencies were secured too late to profit from the living stream, for the stream had already dried up. But the race for colonies, which every historian lists among the tragic events that preceded 1914, was not unconnected with the flow of human stuff out of which colonies are made.

Commerce, finance, foreign markets and colonies — these are factors that no student of modern history can neglect; and in each, migration played a part. Not of least importance is yet another consideration: the influence of the European exodus on the building of the United States. Popular usage recognizes a distinction between those settlers who reached America before 1776 and those who came later. The former are described as "colonists," the latter as "immigrants." In selecting ancestors for social reasons, it is well to have a large proportion of the former among them. A certain work on genealogy states, "It is a relief to know that all members of the —— family were safely in America before the Revolution." The author meant, of course, that the subscribers to the volume were safe for the Blue Book, for membership in the Sons of the American Revolution and the Colonial Dames. The proud descendants were spared the stigma of being the children and grandchildren of immigrants. But in every practical respect the settlers, old and new, were much the same. The Puritan who landed in Massachusetts Bay with his blunderbuss and Bible was an immigrant. The peasant from Eastern Europe who twenty years ago passed through Ellis Island with a pack upon his back was a colonist. They were all colonists, all immigrants. And all were engaged in providing America with ancestors.

In other words, the nineteenth-century immigration was a part of the fundamental process of peopling — the planting of the human breed from which all succeeding generations will spring. Political parties will rise and fall; administrations will be voted in and voted out; issues will be hot and cold; production, distribution, government may be revolutionized; but the stock will be the same — and no one has yet disproved the adage: "Blood will tell." The process of settlement of which immigration formed a part will always remain the first chapter of American history, no matter into how many volumes and appendices the complete work may run.

Something is known as regards the proportions of American blood descended from colonial and from immigrant stock. The application of the quota system to immigration in the 1920's rendered necessary a determination of the "national origins" of the white population. Statisticians and historians engaged in the task of solving this unsolvable problem. The result was: from colonial stock, fifty-one per cent; from immigrant stock, forty-nine.[1] Every step in the computation is open to some objection, but this official estimate represents as close an

---

[1] W. S. Thompson and P. K. Whelpton, *Population Trends in the United States* (N. Y., 1933), 89-91.

approximation as is ever likely to be attained. However, the birth rate of the population representing the forty-nine per cent is higher than that representing the fifty-one per cent, and it will not be long, if the time has not already come, until a majority of the blood of the United States will owe its origin to ancestors who were never American subjects of the British Crown. One still sees in English newspapers references to "our American cousins," but a realistic view must recognize that the degree of cousinship is not close and that it becomes more remote with the continuous process of deaths and births.

The first use of the word "immigrant" seems to date from 1817. The process of immigration was then over two hundred years old, but during the seventeenth and eighteenth centuries the settler was known as an "emigrant." He migrated *out* of something; by 1817 he was migrating *into* something. That something was the new nation which had come into being. Whether in the earlier days or the later, however, the newcomer brought with him no institutions except perhaps that of the family. But he carried the seeds of institutions: likes and dislikes, personal and community customs and habits, and a language or dialect that tended to limit his association to people of his own kind. The historian asks: what was the fate of those seeds? Was the American soil fertile or barren? It is certain that what many immigrants hoped, and many native Americans feared, would happen, did not happen. The country did not develop into a congeries of minorities which made national origin, speech and particular institutions the basis of their political allegiance and activities. But the inquirer wants to know whether this was due to the nature of the social soil (the institutions already existing), or whether the seeds germinated only to be blasted by tempests that swept over the land. In other words, was the outcome inevitable or accidental?

There are, moreover, many phases of life not so obvious as the political in which the millions of immigrants may well have wielded a potent influence. Today there is an American society which, in spite of local and temporary variations, is rather uniform — too uniform, critics say. There are standards of conduct, forms of community activity, ideals of personal success, pastimes and pleasures that are considered American. These are, in many respects, far different from those that prevailed a century ago. But are they as different as one would expect, and did immigration speed or retard the process? By posing this question we enter at once into that dim continent of knowledge called social history, and our groping is the more uncertain because there are so few definite guideposts. In the realm of political history each campaign can be analyzed and the rôle of the foreign-born, or of any group among them, may be determined. The economist who is interested in the past may also hope to reach reasonably satisfactory conclusions as to the effect of immigration upon wages, labor conditions and other definite phenomena. But the historian who is caught in the midst of a social evolution hesitates to pass judgment upon a **process which may have only begun, knowing that, like** the traveler who is following an unknown and winding path, he cannot determine the direction in which he has been moving until he has reached the end.

Yet it is precisely in this field of social evolution that the historian will find the influence of migration the most enduring. Some parallels from other times may clarify this point of view since the nineteenth-century example is but one of the movements of peoples that history records. It must be emphasized that the natural state of population is one of immobility. Even the so-called nomadic tribes were nomadic only within certain bounds and those bounds were, in general, permanent. When for any reason the tribes migrated from an area and overran that of their neighbors, thereby setting them in motion, history was made. When civilization advanced to the agricultural stage, mobility was restricted within even narrower limits and the ties that bound a person to his physical environment were much stronger. In the words of Adam Smith, "A man is of all sorts of luggage the most difficult to be transported." But when the ties did snap and the farmers sought new lands, then also history was made. Mass migration was the result of the break-up of something old and it was the preliminary of something new. It was a sign of change and it hastened change.

To emphasize this principle, let us begin where the anthropologists and archæologists leave off and survey what is called world history in a paragraph or two. Traditionally, "world history" is limited to Europe and its neighboring areas, and it is divided into three periods: the ancient classical world, the Middle Ages and modern times. The early centuries of each of these periods were marked by a shifting of population. When the Greek states first emerged from obscurity, the inhabitants of the ancient world were in motion. They were moving from the islands of the Aegean to the mainland. They were coming down from the north through the Balkans into the peninsula of Greece. They were finding their way from the valley of the Rhine through the Alps onto the plains of Italy. In those ancient melting pots, immigrants and natives mingled and amalgamated to form the Greeks and Romans of history.

The time came, however, when again the population was astir. As early as the era of Cæsar the restless barbarian world was disturbing the frontiers of the empire. Three centuries later the barriers were broken, and first the provinces, and later the imperial city itself, were overrun. For five hundred years history has little to record but the wanderings of these tribes, the destruction they wrought and the temporary governments they and the defenders established. But finally a quiet so profound that tradition has described it as stagnation settled upon Western Europe. Again new peoples and new kingdoms were formed. The medieval age emerged with a culture of its own, an economic system of its own and a distinctive international ecclesiastical organization which tied the parts together.

By the fifteenth century, however, population changes,

which for some time had been under way, made themselves felt. These were more peaceful but of no less significance than those which had gone before. The Germans, steadily advancing to the north and east, occupied the shores of the Baltic and created a northern Mediterranean. The population of the western nations recovered from the losses of the Black Death. Spain finished the last crusade by driving the Moslems back into Africa. Everywhere cities flourished, drawing in the enterprising spirits from the surrounding countryside. Out of the revived commerce and the rivalries that it engendered came the expeditions across the Atlantic and the beginning of modern times. The years from 1500 to about 1900 comprised another grand division of chronology and the nineteenth century was characterized by the greatest migration of all time.

What the period that follows "modern times" should be designated is a problem that can be passed on to the future. Few will deny that a new epoch has begun. The world has become Occidentalized, not merely by ships and armies and money, not merely by colonies and spheres of influence, but by the settlement of European peoples in all lands, north and south, east and west. Migration has set the stage and cast the characters for the next act in the drama. The emigration to the United States was but one phase of a world movement.

Before considering how this one current was influenced by the others, it is well to return again to the distant past for illustrations of the fact that the deeper significance of migration lies in the field of social evolution. Immigration, for instance, did not have any bearing upon the political fortunes of Solon, nor did it account for the Peloponnesian War. But in dealing with the origin of Greek culture it is all important. Was that culture Aegean? Did it come from some mysterious and now forgotten center in the north? Was it indigenous and only modified by the incoming peoples? Whatever the source, historians realize that people are the natural carriers of culture, and the routes of migration must be traced before the most elementary of these questions can be answered.

For understandable reasons, migrations are not the first phenomena to be studied by historians in any field. The first scholars are concerned with chronology. They must reconstruct the time-table of their period. Events and men stand out in all records and, when their dates have been determined, certain points have been established to which everything else may be related. But as this research continues it yields decreasing returns in satisfaction. What good does it do to list the names and dates of more provincial governors, to describe more floods and plagues, to repeat another story of border raids? Those who persist in such labors are likely to be referred to by their fellow scholars as "mere antiquarians." The majority pass on to other subjects, usually politics and diplomacy, and write the history of dynasties and courts. But ultimately historians, like politicians, get around to the "forgotten man." Leaving the palaces, they move down into the slums and out into the fields. As they had once drawn up genealogical tables of kings in order that political evolution might be clear, now they draw up charts showing the descent of the people in order that cultural evolution may be clear.

Until the last half-century the content of what was denominated American history was largely annalistic. Then followed a preoccupation with political, constitutional, diplomatic and military history. There were dissident voices, to be sure, but they were little heeded. The attitude of the majority of professional scholars was natural. The human stuff out of which culture grows was still pouring into the country. Although one might venture an opinion as to the particular contributions of each nationality, no one knew the proportions in which they were represented in the population and no one dared to forecast the ultimate outcome.

Then for five years the World War put a stop to the movement. In 1920 it began to flow again, but the nation had acquired some new ideas and new prejudices, and in 1921 legislation interfered to check the volume. In 1924 the dam was built still higher; and when the national-origins provision went into operation in 1929, it recognized the principle that henceforth those who were allowed to enter should conform to a cross section of the population as it stood in 1920. The balance of foreign ingredients in the American white stock should not be disturbed except by the vitality of the respective nationalities. The melting pot had not completed its work, but the ratio of the cultural elements was roughly determined. It is probably not an accident that general interest in the study of American social history was intensified in the period after the World War and the resulting pause in immigration.

In addition to the perspective of time the historian must also consider the perspective of space. Three population movements of the nineteenth century require attention from the student of emigration. One is the cityward drift, which is as noticeable a feature as emigration. Considered broadly, it is only another aspect of that fundamental division of labor which was the basis of all population changes. Just as continents specialized, so also regions specialized. The factories of the industrial city attracted man power for their enlarged operations from the same European country districts as the large-scale farms of the Mississippi Valley. The son of an English farmer went to Manchester, his brother crossed the Atlantic to Illinois; one German left his native village for Cologne, his neighbor settled in Wisconsin. In general, the emigration from European cities was not great. In those few cases in which it did take place, the loss was more than compensated for by the influx of inhabitants from rural regions. The total population of Ireland decreased about two and a half million in the twenty years from 1841 to 1861, but all the principal cities of the island enjoyed a pronounced gain.

Recognition of this fact narrows the economic landscape upon which the investigator must center his attention when seeking the reasons for the nineteenth-century migration to foreign lands. It was predominantly a rural phenomenon; the emigrant was a son of the soil; his interests were the simple wants and ambitions of the countryman; his vision was limited by the education and intellectual habits of his class; he was aroused to action only by those forces that touched him. These considerations must not be obscured by easy generalities. It has been suggested, for instance, that emigration was merely a phase of nineteenth-century romanticism. Here and there, it is true, a boy read blood-and-thunder stories of the Wild West and soon was listed among the missing. But the head of a peasant family was affected only by the ideas that reached him through the medium of the almanac, the provincial newspaper, the emigrant guidebook, letters from friends who had undertaken the adventure, and the gossip of the village tavern. All had their part in setting the current in motion. Politics has also been ascribed as the motivating factor. Here it must be recalled that most of the political agitation of the century was urban, and peasants had little part in the revolutionary uprisings that marked the advance of democracy. The closer we keep our eyes to the soil, the better the chance of understanding the origin of the emigrants and their reaction to American life.

The second population movement was directed toward Latin America. From the beginning of colonization the tropics had exerted a lure which Europeans found difficult to resist. It was only experience and the presence of competitors that directed English settlement farther and farther to the north. The successful planting of the North American coast, however, did not destroy the earlier interest. The West Indies and the Spanish Main remained the goal of many an adventurous and ambitious youth. But as long as the lands to the south were dependencies of Spain and Portugal and inclosed within their commercial systems, only the exceptional individual could find scope for his energies. With the revolutions in Latin America in the early nineteenth century, the scene changed. New states with boundless lands and untouched resources opened doors and invited exploitation. It was said in the 1820's that the best opportunities in the United States had been seized; what North America was fifty years before, South America had now become. During that decade Brazil was the popular destination of departing Europeans; and in seasons when only two or three hundred Germans entered the United States, two or three thousand were following the longer route to Brazil. This fact illustrates the importance of keeping other migratory movements in mind. He who studies the influx into one country alone has no clear conception of the diverse conditioning factors.

A family that was determined to emigrate studied the map. They looked longingly upon the sunny climes below the equator; they dreamed of plantations and Negro servants, of orange groves and tropical nights. It was all so much more pleasant than the chill winds that swept the forest clearings of North America. Then with a sigh they realized that plantations cost money, that in the tropics a man must import his capital instead of earning it, that political stability was unknown, and that exotic diseases prevailed against which Europeans possessed no immunity. So the more prudent set out for the United States after all. The Brazilian immigrants of the 1820's were not successful, and by 1830 the current was shunted back to the north. Again in the 1850's South America came into favor, with Peru and the Argentine as the promised lands. When disillusionment was once more the outcome, the north regained its repute. Thus the pendulum of popular interest swung back and forth, producing variations in the flow into each country. Although after 1830 the volume to the south never approached that to the north, the periodic renewal of interest suggests what might have happened if internal conditions in Latin America had been more favorable to the type of settler which Europe was then producing in abundance.

The third current of population was toward the British colonies. Of the total number of fifty million European emigrants during the century, thirty-five million sought the United States. Of the remaining fifteen million, nearly ten million settled in Canada, South Africa, Australia and New Zealand. The development of these overseas dependencies markedly affected the character of the British movement to the United States. During the agricultural depression which followed the Napoleonic wars, many of the more prosperous yeoman farmers of England gave up the struggle at home and transferred their households to a land where farming could be carried on with more profit and less anxiety. Until 1830 this class formed an important element of the immigrants settling in the Ohio Valley. They brought with them not only the capital that was so much needed, but also a skill in farming that was unknown to pioneer agriculture. The much publicized Birkbeck settlement in Illinois and the Robert Owen community at New Harmony, Indiana, are only two of the areas in which they congregated.[2] Families and groups of families were scattered throughout the great central belt from Pennsylvania to the Mississippi, and their presence influenced religion, education, philanthropy and politics. Had they continued to arrive in the same numbers, the subsequent cultural evolution of the Middle West would have been along distinctly different lines.

Why this useful class, which had no reason for dissatisfaction with the government of the homeland, should choose the United States rather than Canada, was a question which many a colonial administrator asked. The answer was the comparative difficulty of getting land in Canada and the lack of any positive policy for improving roads and transportation and providing the organs of community life. This situation was changed in the late 1820's by the formation of the Canada Company, which set out to develop its forest empire by offering induce-

[2] M. L. Hansen, *The Atlantic Migration, 1607–1860* (Cambridge, 1940), 94–95, 119.

ments to settlers.[3] The plan worked. Thereafter, the banks of the Ottawa took the place of the banks of the Ohio and Mississippi as the goal of the propertied yeoman farmer. Other advantages being equal, he preferred a home under the British flag. Toward the close of the decade of the thirties political troubles in the provinces tended to deflect the tide back to the United States; but before it attained full flood, the advantages of Australia and New Zealand were brought to public attention by colonizing companies, and the British government's adoption of emigration subsidies tended to equalize the cost of passage and bring the distant colonies within reach. Not until the great agricultural emigration of the 1880's did English farmers again seek the United States in large numbers.

The fluctuations in these migratory movements to other parts of the world help to explain the character of the settlers who went to the United States and the variation in their numbers. The efforts made by other nations and by the British colonies to attract these folk illustrate, by contrast, the strength of the American appeal. But that is not the only reason for keeping these contemporaneous migrations in mind. They provide experiences that by comparison shed light upon American conditions. To understand what happened to Germans or Irish in the United States it is helpful to note what happened to them elsewhere.

[3] M. L. Hansen, *The Mingling of the Canadian and American Peoples* (New Haven, 1940), 109–110.

Two ships left the port of Hamburg a hundred years ago. The passengers came from the same region; they belonged to the same social class; they were provided with equal amounts of worldly goods and brought with them leaders of the same character. The one vessel landed at New Orleans and its passengers proceeded up the Mississippi to the farms of Missouri. The other reached Rio de Janeiro and its passengers proceeded into the southern provinces of the empire. A century has now passed. The descendants of the first group have only a sentimental interest in their origin. If they speak the ancestral tongue it is a result of their school instruction. No distinctions set them off from their neighbors, and they belong to political parties of all shades. But the descendants of the second group, now in the fourth and fifth generations, speak German, think German, vote German. They constitute a Teutonic state in the Brazilian federation. No one, however, has yet explained the reasons for the diversity in social evolution. It is simple to ascribe it to the influence of the surrounding society. The Portuguese did not absorb the newcomers; the Anglo-Saxon did. Therefore the Americanization was an outcome of the superior Anglo-Saxon aptitude for assimilation.

But if we revise the story a little, this explanation fails. As a matter of fact, not two but three ships left the port of Hamburg. One sailed for New Orleans, another for Rio, the third for the port of Adelaide in New South Wales. The passengers on this last expedition founded a community which retained its German individuality with much more tenacity than did that of their Missouri compatriots, and this in spite of the fact that in Australia they were surrounded by an atmosphere more thoroughly Anglo-Saxon. Evidently some other force was at work in Missouri. Any explanation that is propounded for either case must take into account such differences in order to be valid.

Problems of this kind suggest the need for an intensified study of the history of immigration. Amateur interest in this phase of American development is nothing new. Every individual who survived the rigors and hard work of the initial years turned historian in his later days. Written or unwritten, his account was passed on to become the family saga. Migration was an adventure which no participant could afterward view dispassionately. He came from a European village where his ancestors had contentedly dwelt without ever seeing the steeple of the church of the neighboring parish. His routine of existence had been bounded by the landscape, people and customs which had been familiar from birth. He ended up on an American farm, where for the next thirty or forty years the prospect of a trip to town on Saturday afternoon aroused a quiver of excitement. Between the old life in Europe and the new life in America he cherished memories of the last days of departure, the strange traveling companions in the steerage, the excitement of arrival, the mishaps of lost baggage and lost children. It was a six weeks' adventure that the immigrant never tired of telling even when his grandchildren nodded over the tale.

As the years passed and the surviving patriarchs came together, they instinctively formed commemorative societies. Like all men who witness beginnings, they were moved by some inner urge to perpetuate the memory of those significant days. They held meetings, read papers, prepared obituaries for the local newspaper, contributed reminiscences to the county history, and occasionally published pamphlets in which the writings of the year were collected. But these societies did not last long. Death removed the members one by one and, finally, there were no more obituaries to be compiled. Thus ended the first stage in the writing of immigrant history.

While the older immigrants were still considering themselves heroes, the newer ones were being viewed as a problem. That the sociologists took a hand in the recording of this history is not surprising. They were called in to deal with complicated situations that were clearly social: the poverty of a city slum housing a dozen nationalities, or the stagnation of a rural community where some foreign group was living untouched by the forces of progress. As an incident of their work these scholars prepared reports which often contained an introductory chapter entitled "Historical Background." And so in a way they too became historians. They repeated legends, gathered bits of information and occasionally produced a balanced and judicious account of the coming of one nationality or the settlement of another.

It is only in the last twenty years that the topic has become a professional interest of American historians.

This interest has arisen from two sources. One is the increased importance of social history with its all-inclusive outlook. The other arises from the ranks of those who are descended from the nineteenth-century immigrants — persons who consider themselves as American as anyone, though no drop of "colonial" blood flows in their veins. Born with blood that is not British, trained in family institutions that are Continental, speaking very often a foreign language as well as English, these Americans have declared their independence of the traditional history that traces all the roots of national culture back to British soil. They say the sons of the earlier colonists have written their history, now we will write ours.

Unfortunately, when Americans declare independence, they are apt to become rather belligerent about it. Hence, such groups have oftentimes proceeded on the theory that they should claim everything in sight and give up only what is necessary and that grudgingly. If all the pretensions of the Scotch Americans, Irish Americans, German Americans, Scandinavian Americans and the rest are correct, then English influence has been exactly *nil*, for nothing is left. Of course, every writer of such histories finds an audience eager to applaud his most extravagant statements. Politicians deem it wise to fortify themselves with this information before they begin the rounds of their districts. A well-known public official of the city of Chicago has on hand some twenty speeches, each of which deals with the contribution of a particular nationality to American civilization. One is tempted to believe that the only difference between these speeches lies in the substitution of the word Ukrainian for Lithuanian, Italian for German, according to the need. Whether professional historians like it or not, this kind of history is being written and, if they desire to improve its content, their policy should be not to condemn, but to guide these energies into right channels. This has been done in the case of a few nationalities with the result that societies have been organized whose productions meet the highest standards of thoroughness and impartiality.

The historian of immigration can complain of no lack of material. That migration produces an urge for writing, the memoirs and diaries of the founders of colonial New England prove. The later immigrants came at a time when printing presses and paper were cheap. Every man with a mission, with a grievance, or with a simple itch to express himself, bought a press; and Volume One, Number One, soon made its appearance. Over four hundred Norwegian journals have at one time or other been established in America. Milwaukee once possessed six daily papers published in German. The library of the University of Illinois contains copies of American newspapers printed in thirty-three different languages. Some of the immigrant newspapers have existed for more than a century.

The historian who looks upon the thousands of volumes, piled one upon the other, feels like the archæologist who surveys the mounds of Syria or Egypt, knowing that within the débris will be found temples, workshops and homes. Each mound conceals a lost world of routine life that can be unearthed only by spadework of the most laborious and painstaking character. The excavations of immigrant records have only recently begun. Only a few simple outlines of the story are as yet revealed. But what has been found encourages students to dig more deeply. What they have discovered and what they hope to find will make infinitely more intelligible the varied life of America.

II

THE ODYSSEY OF THE EMIGRANT

IT is one thing to consider the transatlantic influx in the large, and another to envisage the story in simple human terms. For each participant the removal to America involved choices, decisions and actions that cut like a surgeon's knife athwart his habitual mode of life. It involved breaking with the ways of his ancestors and oftentimes running counter to the advice of timorous friends. Particularly was this true in the pre-Civil War period when the person concerned might be the first to leave his community and when the journey usually meant travel by sailing craft.

The odyssey of the emigrant began when he first dreamed of the far-off land. Week after week that dream became more real, speculation crystallized into action and, finally, the day of departure arrived. There was a "last" time for everything — a last Sunday in the church with the village pastor extending a special blessing; a last visit to the tavern where the whole company solemnly drank to the success of the undertaking; a last stroll through the winding lanes or along the river's bank; a last night beneath the paternal roof. To hide neighborhood doubts once the decision was made, tradition decreed that festivity should reign. In Germany, orchestras and bands of singers serenaded until the doors were opened and all thronged in for a shake of the hand and a final word of encouragement. In Ireland, where friends felt they were being deprived of what every respectable citizen owed his community — a wake — they proceeded to turn the leave taking into a night of jollification unrestrained by the presence of a corpse. Shortly after sunrise, to the pealing of the village bells, the procession started, accompanied for a mile or two along the highway by the now weeping relatives and neighbors.

When the steeple of the village church disappeared beyond the forest or below the hill, the great adventure was under way. Germans leaving the south of the fatherland usually went by local stage to Strasbourg where, bag and baggage, they were loaded into the cotton wagons returning empty from the factories of Alsace to Paris. After a day or two in the French metropolis, steamers upon the Seine bore them to the port of Le Havre. From north and central Germany, the Elbe and Weser rivers led to the harbors of Hamburg and Bremen. Scandinavian emigrants traveled by land or water to Hamburg, or crossed the North Sea to Hull whence they continued by rail through England to Liverpool. The Irish also usually found it cheaper to take a channel steamer to Liverpool, although at certain seasons vessels bound for the St. Lawrence thronged their harbors.

During the sailing-ship era the entire shipping industry was dependent upon wind and weather. All that an agent could do was to announce a date when the emigrants should be in port, with the warning that the vessel would sail with the first fair wind thereafter. Some arrivals had barely time to make purchases and get themselves on board, but the majority generally idled away from a week to a month. In the search for cheap lodgings these transients sometimes fell prey to sharpers but, in order to maintain the good name of the port, merchants and ship brokers usually found it needful to adopt measures to insure clean and reasonable housing.

The next object of interest to the emigrants was the ship that would convey them to America. Sailors sauntering about the harbor basin willingly pointed out the *Achilles*, the *Sally Ann* or the *Vaterland*; and from the landsman, who knew no boat but the flat canal barge or the ugly puffing steamboat of the neighboring river, the slender lines and trim cut of the craft drew exclamations of admiration and pride. But the emigrant ship was, at best, a puny vehicle in which to brave the waves of the Atlantic. Seldom more than three or four hundred tons in size, it seemed hardly to have room enough for the several hundred passengers which it habitually carried.

Though vessels designed primarily for the emigrant trade made their appearance by the mid-nineteenth century, the majority consisted of cotton, tobacco and timber ships coming back to America in ballast, or of liners and East Indiamen too old to serve their original purpose. The lowest part of the hold contained the heavy baggage and chests, the casks of water and the cordwood used for fuel. Above was the steerage, usually not more than six feet from floor to ceiling, and with no means of entrance but a ladder leading down from a hole in the deck of the hatchway. Around the sides of the steerage ran two layers of berths, cumbersome shelves wide enough for five persons and filling most of the floor space.

Warned by those who had preceded them, most emigrants tearfully disposed of their heirlooms before leaving home, although an occasional German would transport his grand piano or an English farmer his favorite plow and harness.[1] The conditions of the voyage called for a specialized equipment which was secured most cheaply in the ports: a provision box impervious to the gnawing of rats; knives, forks and spoons, a bucket, teakettle, tin cups and plates; a hammer and nails and brass hooks to be screwed into the walls for suspending cheeses, wursts, hams, red herring, onions, bonnets and boots. In addition, enterprising salesmen might persuade the travelers to buy fresh straw for their bedticks, soap that could be used satisfactorily in salt water, and bread baked and toasted to the hardness of ship's biscuit. "Emigrant Provision Stores" abounded in the neighborhood of the docks, where these diversified supplies could be bought already packed. In view of the need for making careful preparation for the voyage, time never hung heavily upon the hands of those waiting in the ports.

The actual moment of embarkation, so long anticipated, usually passed without those philosophic thoughts or

[1] *Morgenblatt für gebildete Stände* (Stuttgart), Oct. 10, 1833; J. H. Gudehus, *Meine Auswanderung nach Amerika* (Hildesheim, 1829), 17.

lofty sentiments that imagination associates with an eternal farewell to Europe. To be at last in motion was a relief. Some of the more active passengers joined with the sailors in heaving the anchor. Others were engrossed with the novel experience of seeing the straining ropes and creaking pulleys spread the sails to the breeze. As the exact hour depended upon the wind and tide, ten or a dozen vessels usually cast loose simultaneously. Hundreds of spectators lined the shore, while scores of rowboats and gigs, with flags and gay banners floating from their improvised masts, speckled the harbor. Handkerchiefs and hats waved incessantly. The air was filled with a babel of sounds: shouts of farewell, happy songs and lively music, occasionally the dull boom of a ship's cannon. Of course, there were some who wept, and a serious-minded clergyman might attempt to emphasize the solemnity of the occasion by a prayer or exhortation. But the most vivid impression was one of a universal joy that caused graybeards and children, men and women, maidens and youths, to dance jubilantly upon the swaying decks. Not until they were beyond the bars and the pilot was let overboard did the majority realize that the world which had given them birth had passed from their view.

When at last the horizon was nothing but water the travelers were mustered upon deck. One by one and, more often, family by family, they appeared before the captain who compared their names with the passenger list, verified ages and, perhaps not too carefully, looked for signs of disease. In the meantime the crew searched every corner of the vessel and usually found stowaways hidden among the water casks in the hold, beneath the heavy berths, or even curled up snugly in emigrants' chests. In German and French ports, where the police surveillance was stricter, the few stowaways were discovered in time to be sent back with the pilot. But detection proved more difficult in the case of ships leaving Ireland. They usually dropped anchor for the night before getting out of the mouth of the estuaries and during this halt friends on shore paid a final visit to those departing. If he had taken the precaution to send provisions aboard by some accomplice, the penniless youth found it easy to secrete himself during these visits; and if his presence were not discovered during the inspection, he would later mingle with the company, his face would become familiar to the sailors, and he would complete the journey without his true identity becoming known.

Cooking facilities on board the vessel were primitive, the equipment being usually placed out on the open deck, completely exposed to the weather. On some vessels this equipment consisted merely of half of a barrel lined with brick and mortar and covered with a grill of a few iron bars. Occasionally there was an ordinary cooking stove but, being completely unsheltered, it generally did not survive the first gale. A few ships were provided with a galley — a small house built on deck, containing an open fireplace probably three and a half feet long. Here three meals a day were prepared for as many as four hundred passengers and by the passengers themselves.

It is an axiom of domestic science that no kitchen is large enough to hold two women, but around this fire a score or more of determined housewives pursued their different culinary purposes. One would be boiling coffee, another preparing a stew, a third with a bowl of batter in hand baking pancakes, when a sudden lurch of the vessel would mix coffee, stew and batter into an unpremeditated combination. Since those awaiting their turn were impatient, the parent was obliged to take the mess to the waiting family as it was, Nature perhaps adding a finishing touch by flavoring it with a dash of salt spray. Very often this joggling of elbows caused a serious physical encounter. No matter how dull life might be elsewhere on board, there was always fighting around the stove, and philosophically minded Germans quietly waiting their turn compared the government to the anarchy of the medieval empire when "*Faust Recht*" alone prevailed. Under such conditions breakfast was not ready until noon and dinner until night; and before the end of the journey both breakfast and dinner might be several days late.

To lessen these conflicts, cooking groups were organized of from ten to fifteen adults, the size varying with the number of dependent children. Very often the members were relatives or persons from the same village, who bunked near one another in the steerage. Their chests and boxes provided tables and chairs, food supplies were put together in a common store, and those physically able took turns at the actual cooking. A committee representing the several groups determined priority in the galley, so arranging the sequence that each would have at least one hot meal a day. On German vessels, where the law required the shipmaster to provide a certain minimum of food, these groups were utilized to assist in its distribution. At five o'clock in the morning a representative of each helped bring up the water casks and fuel and, after aiding in the cooking, carried the portions of the breakfast to his associates in the steerage, returning later to clean the pots and kettles. This routine was repeated at dinner and supper. On many vessels, however, the bread, butter and water were distributed once a week and meat and vegetables once a day, families and individuals being allowed to dispose of their share as they desired.[2] To be conscripted for service in the galley was welcomed by the majority, for leisure bored countrymen who had always been accustomed to an active outdoor life.

All navigators desired to "clear the continent" as quickly as possible, to get away from the headlands and narrow passages out into the Atlantic where by skillful tacking nearly any wind could be utilized to speed the voyage. From Ireland, Liverpool and Le Havre this was comparatively easy to do, although there are instances on record of being "knocked about in the Irish channel for two weeks" and of unfavorable winds holding up a vessel

---

[2] G. M. von Ross, *Getreue Schilderung der Vereinigten Staaten von Nordamerika* (Elberfeld, 1851), 386–387; Friedrich Arends, *Schilderung des Mississippithales, oder des Westen der Vereinigten Staaten von Nordamerika* (Emden, 1838), 19; Friedrich Dellmann, *Briefe der nach Amerika ausgewanderten Familie Steines* (Wesel, 1835), 30; *The Emigrant's Guide to the United States* (London, 1849), 38.

sailing from Le Havre for fourteen days instead of the usual thirty-six hours.[3] It was in leaving the Dutch and German ports that the greatest difficulty was encountered. The natural route was through the English Channel, a passage which emigrants enjoyed because of the alternate sight of the French and English coasts and the presence of fishing boats and cross-channel steamers. But to the seamen it was a constant dread. Dangers lurked in the rocks and shoals on either shore, and only the most direct wind could be put to service. Delays of a few weeks and even of a month were common, which not only upset the ship's time schedule but also depleted the emigrant's stock of food. As a result, many German vessels upon entering the North Sea struck out boldly toward the northwest, rounded Scotland and Ireland, and were helped westward by the drift that finally merges into the Arctic Current. Though a longer route in miles, the chances were good for a shorter passage.

The broad swell of the open Atlantic was greeted with a sense of relief. Life henceforth centered on the deck and in the steerage, but there were constant, if trivial, reminders of the greater world outside. Sometimes it was a sea bird or a leaping fish, a butterfly alighting on the rigging, a mass of weeds or a floating piece of wood. Such occurrences gave rise to conjecture and to amateur dissertations on maritime science. In arousing excitement,

[3] Gustav Löwig, *Die Freistaaten von Nord-Amerika* (Heidelberg, 1833), 32; Citizen of Edinburgh, pseud., *Journal of an Excursion* (Edinburgh, 1835), 8; *The People* (Wortley), I, no. 12, 89; *Pastoral Blatt* (St. Louis), LII (1918), 98.

however, nothing compared with the sight of a distant sail. Spyglasses were directed toward it, and a hundred questions provoked discussion: what nationality, whither bound, what speed was it making? If the ship approached within communicating distance, colors were hung from the mastheads, and on a blackboard placed upon the deck each captain wrote his reckoning of latitude and longitude and noted his port of departure and destination. If both vessels were becalmed, the captains would pay courtesy visits, exchange the gossip of the sea, and perhaps return with some bottles of wine, baskets of fruit or a keg or two of water.

When the ships parted company, life returned to its little orbit. Artisans plied their trade; the shoemaker who had brought his tools and the tailor his needles found employment in serving their fellow passengers. If the vessel was steady, mirrors were hung from every spar and a general shaving took place, while on lines stretched above, the week's washing of brightly colored shirts and petticoats flapped in the breeze. Children ran about, arousing sharp cries of warning as they balanced on rails, slid down the hatchway or ambitiously climbed the dangling rope ladders that led up into the shrouds. Invalids were brought up from below to bask in the sunshine and enjoy the lively scenes of deck life. On days following a storm the sights were especially colorful. At such times, one emigrant wrote in his reminiscences,

The passengers turned out on deck like bees in Spring. Some stand about the stove, cooking, or wait their turn at the fire.

Others take a walk round the jolly-boat, which I may call the ship's farmyard, and talk to the cow, or sheep, or pigs, or poultry in their several tongues; or, they sit upon the water-barrels amusing themselves with a book, or, by the aid of tobacco fumes, wonder what sort of a world it is they are bound for, and build castles in the air.[4]

Sinners and saints lived in close proximity. The gamblers congregated in their corner, tossing the cards from early morning to late at night, while some of their fellow passengers sought release in singing hymns and listening to impromptu sermons. These strange contrasts prompted the lines of a popular ditty:

> We have dancing on the main deck,
> And preaching down below
> We have swearing in the foretop
> As through the waves we go.[5]

There was another side of ship life concerning which the records are less clear. Nevertheless the condition was sufficiently serious to lead Congress in 1860 to pass an act "for the better protection of female passengers," which provided that any officer or sailor on an American vessel who seduced a passenger was liable, if unwilling to marry the girl, to a year's imprisonment or a fine of a thousand dollars.[6] This statute resulted from a petition signed by many persons in New York and Brooklyn, including the mayors of the two cities.

[4] D. Griffiths, *Two Years' Residence in the New Settlements of Ohio* (London, 1835), 13.
[5] Citizen of Edinburgh, *Journal*, 11.
[6] R. G. Albion, *The Rise of New York Port* (N. Y., 1939), 344.

Many passengers found time for neither swearing, preaching, nor amusement. A new life lay ahead and its problems occupied their waking hours. All emigrants had some special bit of knowledge of the New World, derived from letters and personal contacts. The man who had read a book on America was an oracle whose words commanded hushed respect. The sailors, oftentimes natives of the United States, were a constant source of information. Some of the passengers, anticipating their backwoods existence, sat about on deck making miniature log cabins, cutting sticks the proper length, notching the corners, piling them up and covering them with a roof. The most characteristic feature of the floating human hive was the presence of crowds of laughing children. Their liberty and hilarity soon grated upon the professional sensibilities of the schoolmasters among the passengers; and it was not long before a school would be organized in which reading and writing and especially the geography of the new land were taught.

Adults also took time for intellectual pursuits. In the ships coming from the Continent, many of them were eager to learn the English tongue; and as teachers in this branch were usually lacking, in bands or individually they struggled through textbooks and grammars in the hope of gaining at least a rudimentary knowledge of the language with which they must now daily deal. Others, whose minds still dwelt on the bitter injustices of the land which they fled, might organize a debating society which met twice a week, "weather permitting." Many vessels developed the equivalent of a newspaper. Enterprising journalists gathered the events of the day from the crow's nest to the hold, and at a signal the passengers collected upon deck to listen to the reading: news dispatches from Europe, official announcements from the captain, rhymes about the food, and medical bulletins describing the condition of the patients injured in the last steerage brawl.[7]

Such brawls often presented a serious problem. During the first days of the voyage sickness, confusion and novelty kept the unruly spirits subdued; but within a week natural bravado returned, cliques were formed and resentments appeared. When a skillet vanished from its hook in the steerage or a blanket from the bunk or a treasured pound of tea from a chest, someone was guilty and accusations flew fast and furious, usually centering on those whose dialect was outlandish or who had proved quarrelsome over wood or water. So narrow were the quarters that all neighbors seemed intruders, and in the peevish atmosphere differences of opinion respecting the name of a fish or the nationality of a distant vessel often developed into violent altercations. Personal quarrels became group quarrels with the two sides finding handy weapons in the billets of wood stored near the galley and the pokers hung from the stove. Before the mate and the crew could separate the contenders, the deck might be stained with Irish, Scotch, German or Scandinavian blood.

[7] *Morgenblatt für gebildete Leser* (Stuttgart), Aug. 9, 1850.

So chronic were the quarrels that organizations interested in the welfare of passengers attempted to inculcate sentiments of peace in advance of the voyage. Vessels about to leave English ports were sometimes visited by missionaries who distributed tracts and taught the emigrants to sing new verses to the tune of "God Save the Queen," which included the lines:

> In this ship's company
> Let there be unity
> Peace, joy and love! [8]

Hardened shipmasters coöperated by posting strict rules of conduct. All firearms and powder had to be placed in the captain's care for the duration of the trip; and on the principle of the curfew the deck was cleared every night at a stated time and all were forced to descend to their berths and remain quiet. It was a point of complaint that a more rigorous discipline was imposed upon the passengers than was often demanded of the crew. In minor matters the emigrants themselves might assume the duty of regulation. Thus the leader of every eating unit was held responsible for the good conduct of his group. Occasionally a greater degree of self-government was permitted.[9] The passengers would elect a president, a secretary and a court of five which enacted a code of

---

[8] *Emigration and Emigrants* (London, 1848), 6, 52.

[9] P. Schori, *Das Neueste aus dem Staate Ohio in Nordamerika* (Bern, 1834), 9; [J. U. Buechler], *Land und Seereisen eines St. Gallischen Kantonsbürgers nach Nordamerika und Westindien* (St. Gallen, 1820), 18.

regulations with the captain's advice and consent. It devolved upon this committee to sit in judgment upon the violators of the code.

A certain amount of discipline proved necessary for sanitary reasons. There was no medical inspection before embarkation and no one knew what plagues the motley crowd might bring on board. Since disinfecting consisted merely of sprinkling the steerage with vinegar, the most promising precaution was cleanliness. Every morning the second or third mate required the passengers to scrub the floor space about their berths, and often withheld the day's rations until this task was satisfactorily performed. Personal cleanliness was a more difficult matter to enforce. Fresh water was not available for washing clothes, and salt water was a medium to which the majority were strangers. Garments dried slowly and there was always a residue of salt. In their discouragement most of the travelers gave up the effort, continuing to wear the outfit in which they had embarked. Of bathing facilities none existed except those provided by the Atlantic Ocean. When the waves were not running high, ropes were let down from the stern and swimmers were drawn along in the wake. For the less venturesome, a cask upon the forecastle served for early morning ablutions.

The ship authorities placed the greatest reliance on the therapeutic value of fresh air. Every day that the deck was not awash, passengers were obliged to ventilate their bedding, and even the sick were carried above into the sunshine and breezes. If the command were not willingly obeyed, the captain descended into the steerage with pistol in hand, or lowered a blazing tarpot down the hatchway to smoke out the stragglers. Such summary action caused the captain and his mates to be characterized as "tyrants," "despots," "brutes"; and although probably none lived up to the virtues ascribed to them in the public "testimonial cards," it is also likely that few were as villainous as the emigrants' accounts suggest. On only rare occasions did the passengers threaten a mutiny by refusing to carry wood and water. Generally they acted upon the universal advice of the guidebooks that "the captain knows best."

The ocean traveler of today refers to his crossing as "smooth" or "rough," usually experiencing six days of calm or six days of storm. But the two months' passage of a century ago gave the Atlantic an opportunity to reveal all its moods. A period of sunshine was followed by a spell of rain, causing the decks to be cleared and the hatches closed. The several days' confinement in the murky hold, only dimly lit by a smoking lantern and with the air becoming increasingly foul, bred surliness and discouragement among passengers who were so cramped for space that some had to squat in their bunks.

Under such conditions the approach of a real storm afforded a sense of relief, if for no other reason than that it broke the monotony. But relief quickly turned to awe and alarm. Sounds that a peasant farmer had never imagined filled the air: the howling of the wind through the rigging, the moaning of the sea, the sharp commands of the officers and the answering shouts of the sailors, the crying of the children disturbed in their sleep, the sighs and prayers of their elders, the crash of chests wrenched from their fastenings, the constant tinkling of pots and pans swaying from their hooks. With a noise like thunder a wave would break upon the deck and trickles of water would ooze in through the cracks about the hatchway. To many of the anxious passengers, their nerves shattered by the hours of suspense, this was a sign of the approaching end. Even the more optimistic had misgivings when the mate, haggard from loss of sleep, hoarsely called for volunteers to relieve the sailors at the pumps.

Most of the travelers, however, lived to tell the tale and to rejoice that in their odyssey they, like the wanderer of old, could relate "woes suffered in their hearts upon the deep." Every port, it is true, had its roster of missing ships. Few of the vessels, however, met disaster in the open sea; the coasts of Europe and America took the heaviest toll. In shipping circles it was estimated that one out of every hundred Atlantic voyages would end in shipwreck, and that of these wrecks one in twenty would prove fatal to ship, crew and passengers.[10] In the catalogue of horrors the burning of the *Ocean Monarch* off the mouth of the Mersey, the wreck of the *Powhaten* on the Jersey shore and the foundering of the *Charlotte* in the Gulf of St. Lawrence particularly stand out.

After experiencing calm and storm and the wonders of the deep, the emigrant found little novelty in the normal

[10] *Morgenblatt für gebildete Stände*, Nov. 20, 1833.

routine of ship life. Although warned that the passage from Liverpool would last from thirty to forty days and that from the Continent perhaps sixty, he had not anticipated that each day would seem so long. A calendar was chalked upon the ship's deck and as each day closed it was scratched off. But how slowly time passed! Many asserted they had abandoned all hope of seeing the shores of America. Others cursed Columbus that he had ever discovered a new continent to tempt Europeans away from their peaceful villages. Still others found victims for their spleen closer at hand. Surely the captain and his crew were in some way to blame. Every vessel had its amateur navigators who, equipped with a smattering of astronomy, an astrolabe and a chart, made calculations and announced positions with an air of authority which suffered little from being contradicted by the reckoning which the captain posted. If their optimistic assurances did not culminate in a few days in the appearance of land, the captain was no less at fault: he had taken the wrong route, and sullen passengers would point out on the map the course he should have followed, while speculating for what diabolical purpose they were being led astray.

Periods of calm sometimes stretched out into delays with serious consequences. At such times the reserve supply of water was watched with an anxious eye. It was the quantity rather than the quality that caused concern, however. Modern sanitary science is amazed at the casual attention devoted to this necessity of life. It was stored in old sugar hogsheads, in oil casks which had never been cleansed, in vinegar, molasses and turpentine barrels bought at bargain prices in the ports of departure. Even under the most favorable conditions, the contents were almost undrinkable before the end of the journey. On some vessels gunpowder was sprinkled in the barrels as a preservative. This gave the water a blackish appearance and a repulsive taste which increased with time. To make the fluid more palatable, it was sometimes treated with vinegar, or mixed with molasses or treacle; but in the end not even tea, coffee or spirits could disguise the taste.

Although food was not so likely to spoil as water, the danger of a shortage was greater. By his very nature the emigrant was optimistic, and the voyage generally lasted longer than he had expected. Before its conclusion he usually lacked one thing or another. If he had any means, he could purchase from the captain but at prices that diminished his savings for the American adventure. Otherwise his welfare depended upon the charity of his fellow passengers. But this charity proved a precarious reliance because, when the supplies of some failed, the supplies of the others were likely to be near their end and prudence stifled generous impulses. No cases are known of emigrants starving before the eyes of their companions, but the records tell of emaciated and hungry persons falling victim to ship fever, of hard-hearted captains marooning upon the first land that came in sight those whose provisions had given out, and of ships, both passengers and crew, being saved from death by chance meetings with other vessels.[11]

Whether needed or not, the fresh fish available off the Newfoundland Banks proved a welcome relief to the monotonous diet. With the simple tackle at his disposal it was impossible for the voyager to catch any fish outside of soundings; but when the dark blue of the ocean began to change to the light blue of the Banks, ingenious fishermen made hooks from wires and pins and, using lines taken from their chests, settled down contentedly upon the deck to haul in halibut and cod.[12] If a calm or a fog descended, the passengers now uttered no complaint. Even captains, eager to reach port and with a spanking breeze astern, would haul down the sails and lay by for a day so as to permit the travelers this novel diversion.

The relief experienced off the Banks was not due entirely to the greater variety of diet. The Banks meant America and, although hundreds of miles still separated the passengers from their destination, enthusiasm began to revive. Before many days passed the first visitor from the New World greeted them — one of the enterprising pilots who cruised about two or three days off shore.

[11] Citizen of Edinburgh, *Journal*, 50; English Farmer, pseud., *A Few Plain Directions* (London, 1820), 27.

[12] English Farmer, *A Few Plain Directions*, 22; G. Lewis, *Impressions of America and the American Churches* (Edinburgh, 1845), 14; *Hibernicus; or Memoirs of an Irishman, now in America* (Pittsburgh, 1828), 140; W. T. Harris, *Remarks Made during a Tour through the United States of America, in the Years 1817, 1818, and 1819* (London, 1821), 12; T. W. Magrath, *Authentic Letters from Upper Canada* (Dublin, 1833), 66–67.

There was great excitement as his boat approached and a triumphal shout as he stepped on deck. He was welcomed, according to one account, "as though he were an angel from heaven." Now all was life and energy. The lethargy of the voyage disappeared as if the emigrants were already infected with the nervous activity of America. They loosened boxes and trunks from their fastenings and piled them on the deck above; they scrubbed the steerage again, for the first time with enthusiasm, so that there would be no reason for delay when the health officer made his inspection. Beards were clipped and faces shaved; old clothes were thrown overboard; and all dressed in their Sunday best, donning the bright peasant costumes that Americans found such a contrast to their own sober garb. In amazement they looked at one another, recognizing only with difficulty their recent shabby companions.

Even before land came into view, its proximity was evident. Neighboring sails were always in sight and occasionally the blur of a coastwise steamer. The air freshened as the heavy saltiness of the ocean atmosphere was thinned by occasional land breezes. Since most emigrants left home in the spring and approached the New World late in June or early in July, the off-shore wind blowing through meadows, woods and orchards wafted out to sea the fragrance of new-mown hay, or the pungent odor of the forest, or perhaps the perfume of apple and cherry blossoms. With all their senses quickened, emigrants gazed at one another, saying, "Surely all that has been written about America is true and we are at the gates of a Paradise."

The last night on board was devoted to music, singing and dancing. The spirit of friendliness overcame even the most bitter feuds of the voyage. A strange light flashing across the water was greeted with "hurrahs" as the first American lighthouse; and when morning broke, the low green shores assured them that they had reached their new home. Xenophon's men, wrote one emigrant, may have shouted, "the sea, the sea," when the waters of the Euxine lay before them, but with the same enthusiasm he and his comrades cried, "the land, the land." [13]

In the bustling confusion of the day that followed, a few may have longed for the peaceful inactivity of recent weeks. At quarantine the ship was boarded by the health officer, who examined it hastily and looked over the passengers mustered on deck. Undoubtedly whatever benefit his visit contributed was contained in a friendly address of pertinent advice. Such counsel was opportune, for as the vessel passed up the harbor it was surrounded by a fleet of small craft filled with eager, shouting men of business. Some offered alluring bits of silver and copper for mattresses, or bottles and cast-off clothing; others sold newly baked bread and fresh fruits. Agents called for laborers and housemaids, or displayed banners offering lands and farms for sale. Most numerous and active of all were the well-dressed "runners" ready to bear the new-

[13] Griffiths, *Two Years' Residence*, 18.

comers off to hotels and boarding houses, railroad stations and steamship landings.

But of most of the dangers that surrounded them the emigrants were oblivious. New wonders dazzled their eyes and distracted their thoughts. In the good fortune of having reached the land of their dreams few thought of what lay ahead. None knew that three years would see a third of the adults among them in their graves, the victims of the rigors of the climate, of unexpected hardships and of unaccustomed methods of living.[14] They were aware only of a confidence in the future deepened by the sense of dangers already overcome. At the threshold of the New World these Europeans faced the unseen with high faith in themselves and in the country they were joining. They were Americans before they landed.

[14] J. S. Buckingham, *America, Historical, Statistic, and Descriptive* (N. Y., 1841), II, 93.

III

IMMIGRATION AND EXPANSION

THE most persistent theme in American history is the westward march of the people. One may picture the scene as that of an army advancing to the subjection of the wilderness. But this is only a partial view. While the army of pioneers was crossing the continent, another was entering the Eastern ports. Bewildered, often uncouth in speech and shabby in appearance, these new arrivals constituted, in the words of an observing journalist, the "ragged regiments of Europe." They had been defeated by the conditions of life at home and were now seeking an asylum in another continent. For a day or two they remained in the city where they had landed; then silently they passed from view and were swallowed up in the great hinterland.

What became of them there? Did they ally themselves with the pioneers and join in a common attack upon the wilderness? Was their service entirely behind the lines, building canals and railroads to link the frontier with the base? Were they replacements who took over the lands of the natives who moved onward? Or were they invaders who drove the Americans before them? These questions cannot easily be answered. Not until 1850 did the United States census distinguish between foreign-born and native-born; and data have never been collected, for either foreigners or natives, recording the exact place of last residence.

In the absence of exact evidence generalizations must be resorted to. Fortunately, it is not difficult to find contacts between this moving flood of humanity and many of the familiar events of American history. Expansion has been the keynote of our national development. Expansion caused the American Revolution. A growing, restless, energetic colonial people, bursting the bonds of the régime which had been established to regulate their commerce and lands, set up a régime of their own. Expansion helped to bring on the second war with the mother country in 1812, when frontiersmen looked with hopeful eyes on the possible conquest of Canada. But for expansion, a free North and a slaveholding South might have lived together in harmony, smoothing over their difficulties by compromise and diplomacy. West of the Mississippi, however, on the lands belonging to the federal government, the settlers from the two sections came into conflict; and the constitutional question of "slavery in the territories" was the spark which, falling into inflammable material, blazed up into a disastrous civil war.

When that conflict ended, new events and new men appeared on the scene. The major problems now centered in corporations and frauds, antitrust laws and interstate commerce acts, reform movements and new interpretations of the Constitution. But if legislation and judicial decisions seem remote from the world of the cowboy and the homesteader, they none the less resulted from the existence of that world. Corporations regarded as stupendous, when judged by all previous experience, were created to span the continent with railroads and to distribute the products of mine, forest and soil according to a scheme of division of labor operating on an unprecedented scale. Giants were called into being because there was work that only giants could perform. But, as so often happened in mythology, when the work was finished, the presence and appetite of the giants proved an embarrassment. Men who had welcomed them as saviors now cried, "Who will deliver us from these all-devouring monsters?" Only the federal government was strong enough to risk the contest, and the binding and strapping of the corporation has been going on ever since.

In other domains of American history as well, the workings of this factor of expansion may be observed. Society was profoundly influenced by the flexibility and weakness induced by continued growth: intellectual life may be characterized as having been in a state of perpetual adolescence. Constitutional history records repeated adjustments and reinterpretations of a basic law that was drawn up for thirteen states, but was finally stretched to cover forty-eight. Political parties, while retaining their old names, varied their platforms and slogans to embrace the interests of new areas and new groups of population. Diplomatic history deals largely with rival claims to territory and disputes over boundaries growing out of the expansive energies of the people. As a result of this pervasive influence it is not surprising that many of the most striking figures in American biography are those whose careers are entwined with some aspect of nation building. The popular names that a democracy applied to its heroes are strong with the flavor of pioneering: the "rail-splitter," the "wagon-boy," the "pathfinder," the "rough-rider."

Since expansion unlocks most of the problems of American history, to appraise the significance of immigration we must know its relation to this great motivating force. But before seeking to clarify this mystery another and less tangible aspect of expansion must be examined. Out of it has arisen an interpretation of American development which has been taken from the historian's study and installed in the executive offices of the government. The frontier theory has ceased to be merely a theory: it has become the basis of a program of action.

Frederick Jackson Turner, the formulator of the classic expression of this theory, has revealed its inception. As a graduate student in the Johns Hopkins University, he listened with skepticism to the dictum of the professor who declared that, to understand the origins of American institutions, one need only concern himself with those centuries during which European institutions were taking shape. America, in other words, had created nothing new — it had merely borrowed. Turner's fellow students therefore wrote dissertations on the Germanic origins of New England towns and found vestiges of the Anglo-

IMMIGRATION AND EXPANSION

Saxon witenagemot in colonial assemblies. The student from Wisconsin, however, was not convinced. In the frontier town of his birth and boyhood he had seen institutions in the making, and his dissertation dealt with "The Character and Influence of the Indian Trade in Wisconsin." A few years later, in 1893, when the ideas foreshadowed by his dissertation had matured, they were elaborated in his well-known essay, "The Significance of the Frontier in American History."

In what respects, asked Professor Turner, has American development differed from that of contemporary Europe? He found the answer in the presence of an empire of land that awaited occupation. It was this land which made the ideals of democracy a reality. The American was given not only a belief in equality, but a generous slice of the public domain with which to maintain equality. Such land was always available in the border region between the wilderness and the more fully matured communities of the settled districts. This transition area was the frontier and it exerted its influence through the presence of free land. For the first hundred years of the Republic that influence was potent. No given area long remained in the frontier stage. The process of settlement was rapidly accomplished when once the pioneer invasion began. But no sooner was the conquest completed than a new frontier appeared upon the horizon, and what had once been "West" now became "East." So the man who had failed in business, the farmer with a half-dozen sons whom he did not want to see sink to the status of laborer or tenant, could start anew on the frontier. Land monopoly was impossible and the formation of a distinct industrial class was discouraged by the abounding opportunities. When depression threatened to culminate in social unrest, it was the frontier which acted as a safety valve by drawing off the disturbing elements.

Turner pointed to the significance of the assertion made by the Director of the Census of 1890 that the frontier had at last disappeared. This meant the era of free land was over: the first period of American history, that of settlement, had come to an end. Then, turning to the future, the historian raised the question: if the existence of "free land" has hitherto preserved democracy and equality and prevented social stratification, what do the years ahead hold, and by what new measures can the loss be compensated for? He offered no answers.

In time, his followers extended and confirmed the thesis; and as they assumed positions of authority in the academic world, instruction in the frontier theory became part of every orthodox course in American history. Turner was well aware that he was stating a broad hypothesis which would need qualification and modification as new evidence appeared; but to drive home his point of view, he simplified what he knew. His disciples further simplified the idea in order that their undergraduate listeners might understand. Many of these became instructors in secondary schools, and they simplified it even more for the sake of their pupils. Consequently, there has come to maturity a generation of Americans who, if they have forgotten everything else about the past, know that once the frontier meant opportunity; and a surprisingly large number of them believe that all opportunity in the United States ended with the census of 1890.

Before Professor Turner died in the spring of 1932, he had the satisfaction of knowing that his contribution to historical interpretation was generally accepted by scholars. But he did not know that exactly a year later there would be legislation guided by men who had adopted the disappearance-of-free-land thesis as the historical justification of their program. Without Turner's frontier theory, the New Deal would have been politically much more difficult to achieve, for its philosophy reconciled many to the belief that the manifold measures undertaken to aid the underprivileged would restore by law an equality that formerly had been guaranteed by the conditions of American life. Whether Turner's view was right or wrong, whether the resulting legislation has been good or bad, there is no doubt that the theory is a living force. It was an outgrowth of the process of expansion, and in that expansion the immigrants were involved. What part did they play?

The abundance of land to the west did not necessarily mean settlement, certainly not settlement at the speed with which it actually occurred. Many of the motives for migration did not exist in the East; the westward advance was not inevitable. On the contrary, many positive factors in the older settled regions might well have acted as a hindrance to the movement. The American had no desire to be neighbor to the Indian; the war whoop and the tomahawk were realistic enough in grandfathers' tales. The fevers and agues that visited pioneer clearings were also well known. Moreover, the journey was long and costly, at least in time and supplies. The planting of one season was lost and a year of hand-to-mouth living was inevitable.

What hastened settlement was the mobility of the Americans as compared with other peoples. The available land was seized upon with an avidity that illustrates the restlessness of the people as well as the opportunities of the frontier. Mobility was an early acquired trait commented upon by many observers. In America, writes the Norwegian novelist, Knut Hamsun, in his bitter book about the New World as he saw it in the eighties, "every day is moving day, and the noise and confusion that are associated with moving in and out are heard and seen constantly in the streets. The population is only half-settled."[1] Nor did this instability affect merely city dwellers. Other Europeans were surprised, even shocked, at the sacrilegious attitude of agriculturists toward the "holy earth." The farms hewn from the wilderness were not to be homes for untold generations of descendants; they were sources of income with which the owners would willingly part if they scented a speculative gain in the transaction. They traded farms in the same light-hearted spirit that they swapped horses.

[1] Knut Hamsun, *Fra det moderne Amerikas aandsliv* (Copenhagen, 1889), 2.

Two reasons for this mobility have been advanced: a migratory habit which characterized the people, and the kind of agriculture they practiced. Undoubtedly both reasons operated, and each deserves fuller consideration. Evidence of the migratory habit derives principally from anecdotes recorded by none too friendly visitors. The instinct urging the Yankees to move on was reported to be so irresistible as to warrant the saying: "If hell lay in the west they would cross heaven to reach it." Aversion to neighbors encouraged the impulse. Every local history tells of the pioneer who departed hastily when he learned that another family had settled in the vicinity. The distant sound of a rifle or the smoke of a camp fire — signs betokening the arrival of newcomers — caused him to hurry to his cabin, whistle to his dog and be off. Even the more sociable individual was easily set in motion. With so much land to choose from, one could never be content with what he happened to possess. Somewhere was a perfect hundred-and-sixty-acre tract: the right balance of meadow, arable and forest, a clearer spring, a more sheltered spot for his home, more wild game in the woods and fewer snakes and crows. He heard that conditions were better in Ohio, then in Illinois, then in Kansas — and he tried them all. For forty or sixty years he wandered in the wilderness in search of the Canaan that he believed existed.

For Yankee youth, migration became the normal experience. Therein lies an essential difference between native and foreign-born. The ambition of the German-

American father, for instance, was to see his sons on reaching manhood established with their families on farms clustered about his own. To take complete possession of a township with sons, sons-in-law and nephews was a not unrealizable ideal. To this end the would-be patriarch dedicated all his plodding industry. One by one, he bought adjacent farms, the erstwhile owners joining the current to the farther West. Heavily timbered acres and swamp lands which had been lying unused were prepared for cultivation by patient and unceasing toil. "When the German comes in, the Yankee goes out," was a local proverb that varied as Swedes, Bohemians or other immigrant groups formed the invading element. But the American father made no such efforts on behalf of his offspring. To be a self-made man was his ideal. He had come in as a "first settler" and had created a farm with his ax; let the boys do the same. One of them perhaps was kept at home as a helper to his aging parents; the rest set out willingly to achieve beyond the mountains or beyond the river what the father had accomplished in the West of his day. Thus mobility was fostered by family policy.

Equally important as a predisposing factor was the type of agriculture that prevailed. The pioneer farmers burned down the trees because it was the easiest way to make a clearing. They planted the same crop, season after season, largely because they were mentally too sluggish to experiment with new products. As a result, the soil became impoverished and no attempt was made, either by scientific rotation or by fertilizing, to restore or maintain its productivity. The land was mined, not farmed, and when the surface treasures had been skimmed off, the process was repeated in another place where Nature's bounty was as yet untouched.

Wasteful though these methods may seem today, a good word should be said for the pioneers. In the onward sweep of population they performed an indispensable task. Without their services as a vanguard, the great army in the rear could not have occupied the two and a half thousand miles from the Alleghenies to the Pacific in less than a century. Some may say that such a planless sprawling over the continent should have been prevented anyway. Perhaps it should, but then an entirely different national policy would have been necessary, in which case the frontier farmer was no more to blame than the Presidents and legislators who failed to adopt such a course.

This rapid agricultural conquest was achieved only by a division of labor which the successive stages of frontier development reveal. Little needs to be said here about the first comers: the professional trapper and the Indian trader. They were followed by the true frontiersman. His equipment was an ax, a rifle, a knife and a frying pan. He built a cabin, chopped down the trees on an acre and did a little scratching between the stumps. He cleared out a spring and cut a trail to the river. Though he raised a little Indian corn, in reality the forest furnished his table: deer, wild turkey and fruits in season. Perhaps he had a horse that pastured itself, but of other livestock he had none. Then one day he heard the distant rifle shot and he resolved to move on, not necessarily because he disliked society, but perhaps because game was becoming scarce and too many rifles would destroy what remained.

His place was taken by the pioneer farmer, who brought a family, more tools and some cows and pigs. The one-acre clearing was expanded to ten or fifteen. The patch of corn was increased and wheat and oats were planted. The farmer added peach and apple trees and a vegetable garden tended by his wife. He turned the spring into a well and broadened the trail into a road. His cattle and hogs foraged for themselves until the autumn round-up; then they were slaughtered, and the sons set out for Cincinnati or went farther down the river to New Orleans to exchange the pork and beef for clothing and powder, or sell it for dollars and cents. The pioneer farmer needed money, for he was no squatter. A payment for land was due the government and taxes must be met. To keep ahead financially was a difficult matter and it was the lot of many ultimately to "go under." One season the cattle would eat a poison weed, or there would be no market for pork, or the blight would destroy the wheat. Debts became heavy, leading to the decision to sell and start over again in a different place.

So the pioneer in turn disappeared, to be succeeded by the permanent farmer who could afford to pay cash for the land and improvements. He also raised cattle and hogs, but he housed them in stables and pens, where he fed them on the products of the field. More land was cleared; and wheat, carried to the mill, was sold as flour in the near-by city which had sprung up in the wake of the advancing host. Many of his sons moved on, but he was content to remain thirty or forty years until at last his bones rested in the community cemetery.

The frontiersman hunted in a region for perhaps ten years; the pioneer farmer held on for another ten. But it was characteristic that with every decade each group shifted one stage forward. No wonder observers thought that the Americans were only half settled and that the national character required them to be ever on the move.

To these two basic causes for mobility — national tradition and agricultural methods — a third should be added: foreign immigration. Without the influx of millions of Europeans, this clocklike progression across the continent could not have occurred. The population would not have been so mobile. There would have been a frontier, to be sure, but not the kind of frontier that produced the now accepted historical consequences. At what point did the immigrant of the nineteenth century contribute his capital, his strength and his skill? The European newcomer was not, in the American sense, a frontiersman. He had, in fact, an innate aversion to the wilderness with its solitude and loneliness and primitive mode of life. Moreover, the job of frontiersman was a highly skilled profession, involving a thousand knacks and devices by which Nature's raw materials were transformed to satisfy the demand for food and shelter. It called for aptitudes that were not developed in the

European village. Neither by experience nor temperament was the immigrant fitted for pioneering.

If many at first intended to emulate the backwoodsmen of whose thrilling exploits they had read in American works of fiction, the resolve generally faded upon the first acquaintance with the strange new world and upon learning that the backwoods lay far from the port of debarkation. Those who nevertheless pursued their original intention soon regretted their temerity. The boundless forest was a disheartening sight, and the American ax a dangerous instrument in the hands of a novice. After the first tree was felled with painful toil, the forest still loomed dense and gloomy; and the knowledge of all the labor that must be expended to clear each acre for corn and wheat deepened the feeling of discouragement. The experience was one they shared with the colonists of two centuries before, as Captain John Smith indicated when he wrote that in the primeval forest of Virginia every third blow of the ax was drowned out by an oath. Of the immigrants who ventured into the wilds few made a success. The majority drifted back to civilization; and their advice, spread by word of mouth, by letters and by printed guidebooks, was emphatic: let the Americans start the clearing; they alone possess the specialized technique.

This advice was heeded. The first white man to pioneer in any township was not a Schultz or a Meyer, a Johnson or an Olson. He was a Robinson, a McLeod or a Boone. He was a descendant of that old Americanized stock which had learned frontiering in the difficult school that was in session from 1600 to 1800. This stock remained in the van when the stream of settlers pressed on through the mountains and into the central valley.

But if the immigrants were not frontiersmen, did they not constitute a large proportion of the second class, those who have been described as pioneer farmers? Among these later comers a number were found, but not a large percentage and only a few of these were recent arrivals in America. At this stage backwoods duties still predominated; handling the ax was more important than holding the plow. Nor did the German or the Irishman know how to preserve meat for the New Orleans market, or how to pilot a flatboat over river rapids. Therefore he tended to avoid this stage of frontier development, leaving it to the natives or at least to those foreigners who had served an apprenticeship on an American border farm, where they had forgotten everything about European agriculture and learned much that was new.

It was when the pioneer farmers departed that the immigrant farmers made their appearance. In the 1820's and 1830's they took over the evacuated lands in western New York, Pennsylvania and Ohio. In the 1840's they swarmed into Missouri, Illinois and southern Wisconsin. In the 1850's and 1860's they occupied eastern Iowa and Minnesota and consolidated their position in the older states. By the 1870's they had reached the prairies. And while the immigrants were moving in, the Americans were moving out — not all of them, but enough to give the invaders an opening wedge which they spread quietly and steadily in the subsequent decades.

These generalizations, of course, are somewhat oversimplified. At times the three stages of frontier development possessed the clear lines of demarkation that have been suggested; but perhaps just as often they shaded into one another, or the stages overlapped. Sometimes within one geographic unit all three stages were being experienced simultaneously. It is, therefore, easy to find exceptions. The possibility of exceptions was increased by the customary method of immigration by families. What should have happened to the economic man according to the usual rules did not occur because the individual was lost in the family, and the economic family dulled the edge of many of the law's decrees.

The resources of the family were pooled first to facilitate transportation across the Atlantic, and then to acquire a landed estate in America. The family migrated piecemeal if, as often happened, the funds were sufficient to send only one member across the sea. The eldest son departed and found employment. In a year his savings paid for the passage of his sister, who entered domestic service. Within two years their combined savings brought over the parents and the other children. In a similar fashion, when the family were all safely in America, they were likely to scatter and each work at the job for which he was suited. The father engaged in day labor in the East, the daughters went into service, while the eldest sons set out for the West, took up pioneer agriculture, and finally reunited the family whose joint savings tided the farm over poor seasons that otherwise might have proved disastrous. All such circumstances modified the transition from stage to stage. The imagination can readily provide a score of variations.

In the great majority of cases, however, especially in the early years of an immigrant group, the newcomers bought farms that were already cleared. To do this they had to have money, and a considerable amount for persons who had only with difficulty been able to pay for the ocean passage. The transaction, therefore, involved postponement of the ultimate ambition. Meanwhile they dug canals and built railroads; they excavated foundations and constructed factory dams; they quarried rocks, made bricks and mined coal. Living in tenements of the meanest sort, they hoarded every penny and added it to the family fund. Then, when business activity began to slacken and jobs became scarce, the family went west and with the cherished savings bought a farm at a depreciated price. This process was well understood. Even agricultural immigrants came to America in greatest numbers at times when industrial activity was at its height; their westward movement was always strongest in periods of depression.

Once a foreign community was established in the West, a new factor affecting distribution made itself felt. The historian of the nineteenth century notes the growing exchange of commerce between Europe and America, the cross currents of literature and religion, the speeding up of communications, the growth of common ideals of democracy. These ties, multiplying from decade to decade, drew the continents together and consolidated an Atlantic world of politics and culture. But no tie was so close, no connection so strong, as that woven out of the millions of personal strands binding remote American townships to secluded European villages. The first person to set forth from one of these villages was attended by the thoughts and dreams of scores of neighbors. In after years he was still recalled by old residents as a sort of legendary character. The first member of a family to venture on the journey long continued to be the principal topic of conversation around the fireside. At scenes of parting the last admonition to be called out was, "Write soon!"

And he did. The rising curve of emigration is paralleled by the increasing number of letters sent eastward over the Atlantic. These letters usually were brief, simple dispatches from the front. Suppose only one of the thousands of mail pouches of 1840 had been undelivered and today were found hidden away in a warehouse in Liverpool or Amsterdam, what a realistic picture of a century ago the yellowed sheets would reveal! Every line breathed a direct message from one human being to another; every report spoke the unvarnished truth of things as the writer had experienced them; every bit of advice sent to the brother who was to follow constituted a sacred commandment. In such a household the far country ceased to be a vague geographical designation. America was not New

York, but a distant crossroads village; it was not Boston, but a forest clearing or a labor camp twenty miles from a post office. When a second member of the family set off, he directed his steps to that locality.

By accretions of this kind the settlement grew, causing the orthodox process of frontier succession to function with less regularity. The farmer who had made good wrote to his former neighbor, "I know of eighty acres not far away, for sale cheap. They are heavily timbered without improvements, but you can live with me and help me with the chores until you get your own place ready." Or the letter read: "My Yankee neighbor wants to move; he is asking ten dollars an acre for his farm, but it will spare you the trouble of starting in the woods. The bank will lend the money, and I will go security on the note." Assistance of this kind became traditional, and was so much taken for granted that newcomers appeared unbidden and at most unseasonable times. In the autumn darkness the farmer might hear a knock on his door and open it to see a group gathered by the roadside, perhaps a former schoolmate and his family of whose coming he had had no warning. But according to immigrant ethics he took care of them. Clergymen lay under a special obligation. The parsonage tended to be both a hotel and an informal employment agency.

Community overpopulation was likely to be the result. Relief was found only when the colony sent out a subcolony or, more often, half a dozen. Young men who had reached maturity in America, fathers who had become infected with the prevailing restlessness, established themselves elsewhere, usually not more than a score of miles away. The main colony became fringed with a group of satellite colonies which continued to trade and attend church in the old community. In turn, each of these centers attracted the newly arrived. Yankees were bought out and new lands opened. What the map had once shown as a large spot surrounded by smaller spots grew together into a blotch — a settlement with a dozen churches where English was the foreign tongue.

When this large settlement in turn became crowded, colonies were sent out to more distant regions, perhaps across state boundaries. The migration often assumed the form of a joint enterprise. A caravan of a hundred or more wagons departed and took possession of a township. Additional immigrants, however, usually continued to seek the old communities, where they were told that ampler opportunities awaited them in the newer settlements. So they resumed their journey, generally with more hardships; and the story of surprise arrivals and enforced charity was repeated. A decade passed and again the social organism divided, losing perhaps a little of the original homogeneity at each division.

By 1870, when the policy enacted in the homestead law was beginning to operate, new material conditions and mental attitudes governed the process of expansion. The powerful appeal of free farms overshadowed caution and lured the immigrants at once to the frontier, for they wanted to get there before the land was all gone. Broadly speaking, the homestead area corresponded with the great triangle that is included between the upper Mississippi and the Missouri rivers, with an extension westward of the latter in its lower reaches. South of this region there was some public land, but it was either in the hands of the Indians or of poor quality; to the west lay barren plains and the mountains; to the east much of the country was already occupied under previous laws. Hence within this triangle occurred the principal concentration of immigrants during the seventies and eighties: the Scandinavians, the Germans and the English. That most of them survived to people this section with their descendants today is no indication of the struggle they passed through as pioneer settlers.

Unfortunately they did not understand the conditions necessary for successful farming in this new country. The homestead was free: any American citizen of legal age, or any foreign-born person who had declared his intention of becoming a citizen, might secure a deed to a hundred-and-sixty-acre tract of his own choice by living thereon and cultivating a part of it for a period of five years. But in other respects they soon learned that the homestead was not free. Though the land was provisionally theirs, the sod had to be broken, and an ordinary plow was torn to pieces by the matted roots of prairie grass. Breaking the sod was a skilled job, and it cost the homesteader two or three dollars an acre to have it done. Since there were no springs and few streams, a well was an indispensable but expensive improvement. But this was not all. The livestock had to be watered and, although the farmer owned only a few head, he could not spend the needed hours in pumping: a windmill was requisite. Moreover, Nature had failed to provide the materials for fencing, and a few acres at least must be inclosed. For this purpose building materials had to be imported, and even the rudest shelters for home and stable cost an appreciable sum. It was usually estimated that a thousand dollars was the capital necessary to make a homestead worth having.

But what immigrant had a thousand dollars upon arrival? Those who did were generally wise enough to settle in the older states where the homestead stampede, which also affected the natives, created many an opportunity for judicious buying. The penniless ones who made the attempt were willing to agree, before they had spent the first winter in a sod house with little fuel and no livestock, that the frontier was no place for the immigrant. That many deserted is indicated by the difference between the number of official homestead entries and the number of claims that were "proved up." It was a struggle in which the casualties were heavy; and those who were defeated turned back to the industrial cities and older agricultural communities, where there was the possibility of a wage or at least of charity.

That more did not retreat was due to a provision of the law and to certain opportunities for employment. Although the statute required five years' residence, up to six months in any year might be spent elsewhere. It was a saving clause. The six months away could be devoted to labor, and the earnings made possible continued improvements. Wherever work was to be found, far or near, there the impoverished homesteader traveled. Fortunately, for those who had strength and could endure hardships, opportunities offered that were not remote. To the northeast lay the "big woods" of the upper Great Lakes — the pine forests of northern Minnesota, Wisconsin and Michigan. For the lumber that this region produced there was a continuing demand. Every prairie home was built of boards cut from the logs floated down to the mills; the cities were collections of wooden boxes, large and small. In the rapidly settling West a million new homes had to be furnished with three or four million chairs, a million tables, a million cradles. At the beginning of winter an army of choppers invaded the forests and remained until the snow changed to slush. This army was recruited from the homesteads, departing when the harvest had been gathered and returning before the spring labors began.

Nearer by were the railroads. The building of a transcontinental line was an epoch-making achievement, but the road was profitless without feeders. To this end, parallel lines, one after the other, were constructed to branch off from the main stem. Hardly more than twenty miles apart, they tapped the wheat belt by bringing nearly every cultivated acre within a day's wagon journey of a grain elevator. These branches the homesteaders built by working during the late summer in the lull that preceded the harvest; and the services of man and beast were paid for by those corporations against which the farmers were in later years to turn with such bitterness. In one other respect the railroads were a boon. They also had grants of land from the government, better located and usually more fertile than the homesteaders' claims. Prosperous settlers with capital to invest bought these lands and created estates sometimes hundreds or thousands of acres in extent; and at seedtime and at harvest the homesteader could there earn a welcome daily wage.

In this fashion immigrants and native Americans who came into this region without resources earned the sums that were necessary for success. They knew neither the independence nor the self-sufficiency that the earlier frontiersman had enjoyed. Their hardships may have been as severe and their courage as great, but as a historical type they formed a special class of their own.

In summary, just what was the influence of immigration upon American expansion? By nature and habit the American was restless. Undoubtedly he was destined to inherit the earth from the Atlantic to the Pacific. But, as the evidence shows, he was hastened into his inheritance. When an Englishman or a German came with gold in his hand and asked, "Will you sell?" there was no hesitation in the reply. He took the gold and went. Thus the immigrants were the "fillers in," and by virtue of the numbers and speed with which they came they helped to give the movement of expansion its disorganized and reckless character.

IV

IMMIGRATION AND DEMOCRACY

OF all historical interpretations the political is the simplest. Many contemporaries who attempted to explain the rage for emigration attributed it to discontent with political conditions in the homeland. They admitted that the motive of the penniless laborer or the small peasant might be primarily economic: his lot could hardly be worse and it might be made a great deal better. But the emigrants were not all of this element; a large proportion represented that uncertain rank in society described as the middle class. They took with them some pieces of gold and chests of personal property; they were accustomed to a standard of living that would be difficult to reproduce in the backwoods or on the prairie. What could they be seeking that their native country did not provide? It must be political liberty.

The truth is that an emigrant's motives were usually mixed. Before leaving home, when making application to local officials for permission to depart, he emphasized the material: the difficulty of providing a living for his family and the fear that they might be thrown upon the community for support. If the parish clergyman urged him to hesitate before risking everything in such a perilous adventure, the father pointed to his sons who were becoming lazy and shiftless in a country that could give them no work. Hence emigration was represented as a moral tonic. When he met his friends in the village tavern, where everyone grumbled about taxes and unsympathetic officials, he spoke of freedom as his purpose.

Upon arriving in America, however, two of the three motives were likely to be forgotten and the third emphasized. No longer did he mention material incentives. To do so would confirm the belief of the natives that the foreigner was a dangerous economic competitor, and their welcome would curdle into suspicion. Nor did he say that his sons needed moral discipline, for this would give point to the argument that immigrants were depraved and worthless. But one sentiment the American loved to hear. Still affected by the colonial's sense of inferiority, he believed that in culture and in wealth his country did not compare with the older nations of Europe. He did have his Constitution, however, and that was his constant boast. Hence when the newcomer said, "I came to the United States to enjoy the blessings of your marvelous government and laws," the native warmed to him and was likely to inquire whether there was not something he could do to assist him.

Immigrants soon learned the magic charm of this confession of faith. They seized every opportunity to contrast the liberty of the New World with the despotism of the Old. They accepted the invitation to become naturalized as soon as the residence requirements permitted, and with the enthusiasm of converts they praised the Republic and the material blessings it offered. Without doubt most of them were sincere. They did not stop to analyze the chief reasons for their worldly success — harder work and ampler natural resources — but repeated what it was pleasant to say and pleasant to hear. So the tradition was established, and the desire for political freedom was accounted one of the principal causes for the immigration of the thirty-five million Europeans.

Contemporaneously the same view was being publicized in the countries from which the new citizens came. The leaven of democracy was working in every state of Western Europe. It was a powerful force; but the obstacles were many and the champions of reform mustered every argument that the present and the past suggested. At first, the political agitators could make little point of the departure of a few thousand subjects; the conservatives merely said, "Good riddance." Then the thousands increased to tens of thousands; and as landlords lost tenants and had to pay higher wages, they tried to stop the stampede by curbing the activities of the passenger agents and emphasizing the miseries of emigrant life. At this juncture the reformers said, "It's no use; you must go to the root of the matter. These people want larger political rights and, if they can't get them at home, the Atlantic won't stand in the way of their desires."

The political factor cannot be denied, but it must not be exaggerated and must be more closely defined. Among the recurrent movements, that from Germany in the 1850's is popularly classed as distinctly political. The revolutions of 1848 were followed by reaction, and reaction was accompanied by emigration. The grandchildren of these Germans usually say it was despotism that sent their ancestors to America. But when the facts are studied impersonally and collectively, the investigator cannot escape the conclusion that the areas of political disturbance did not coincide with the areas of emigration. From the cities that had witnessed bloody street fighting the emigrants were few; from the peaceful country districts the departing throngs threatened to depopulate the land. Carl Schurz and his fellow political refugees were the exceptions that proved the rule. Numbering perhaps a few thousands, they represented but a small fraction of the more than a million Germans who reached America during the fifties.

When the professional revolutionists talked about liberty, they had in mind republican institutions and guarantees of free speech and a free press. But this was not the conception of liberty cherished by the average emigrant. European settlers in America have seldom shown any pronounced antipathy toward monarchy as such. Most of them retained a genuine affection for the ruling houses of their respective countries, and it was by no means exceptional for them to hang in the living room a print, sometimes only a newspaper illustration, of the monarch whose allegiance they had forsworn. Even free speech meant little to persons who had few opinions to express, or a free press to those who could only with difficulty write their names.

The freedom they sought was of a different sort. Parliaments and courts were miles away, but there were despots at home whose iron hand rested upon the peasants far more heavily than any decrees of a distant government. This sentiment runs through the documents that reveal the popular grievances of the time. What poor people wanted was freedom from laws and customs that curbed individual economic enterprise. In the cities they wished to escape the regulations of guilds and trade unions; in the country they sought exemption from traditional restrictions upon the transfer of land, the working at a trade, or the conduct of agriculture. In other words, they wanted the freedom to buy, sell and bargain, to work or loaf, to become rich or poor. Little wonder that free enterprise was the thought that predominated when immigrants reported the blessings of the New World. "What I like about the country," wrote a Swede, "is that the farmer can dismiss his hired hand any day he wants to, and the hired hand can leave when the impulse strikes him. As a result, each is more careful with respect to the other than in countries where the terms and conditions of service are drawn up in a legal contract."

This freedom was deemed the source of individual energy and of social well-being — the hidden spring of that transformation which in the course of a generation would replace the wilderness with the institutions of civilization. To enjoy the opportunities of free enterprise and to preserve the fruits thereof — this was the aspiration of the rank and file of immigrants. Republicanism and monarchism were only shadowy backgrounds to something more personal and vital. Hence, the system they found in America was one they wished to preserve. As a result, the weight of immigrant political influence has historically been felt on the side of conservatism.

Intelligent European observers often described the emigrants as belonging to the "anxious classes." Few were obsessed with fantastic illusions as to the wealth that awaited them. The bulk of them merely hoped to preserve what they had — not alone property, but a status in society which was uncertain at home. Independent artisans feared a step downward into the ranks of factory workers; tenant farmers dreaded the fate of landless agricultural laborers. All thought that in the New World they could win through to success. They did not want to level down the gradations of society; they had no ideas of dividing up wealth; they were not socialists or communists. Usually they were democrats, but only in the sense that they believed that the American brand of government would facilitate the acquisition of property and position and would protect them in what they had acquired.

Undoubtedly this attitude was strengthened by the proneness of most expatriates to cling closely to the folkways of the old countries. A few years ago two scholars from the University of Oslo went from one Norwegian-American settlement to another, taking phonographic transcriptions of current speech. The recordings showed that words, accents and even dialects which had disappeared from the motherland were in daily use in the prairie communities and that the second and third generations were perpetuating usages that would otherwise have been archaic. The history of the English language in America illustrates the same tendencies of immigrant speech. In the mountain valleys of the South, which were settled in colonial times and into which no recent stocks have penetrated, old English expressions and popular ballads have been handed down from post-Elizabethan times.

Religion reveals another aspect of this conservatism. A bookseller in Bergen, having stocked many copies of a hymnal which had been superseded in the Norwegian churches, sent them all to his agent in the United States who quickly disposed of them to congregations that would use no other. Devotional books which are now to be obtained only in antiquarian shops in Norway are continually reprinted by the Lutheran publishing houses in America. Ministers and synods of immigrant churches have always been less liberal in theology and ecclesiastical practice than the brethren they left behind; and laymen who before emigration had had only a casual connection with the church entered with enthusiasm into problems of congregational finance and orthodoxy.

What influence did the presence of immigrants have on American democratic institutions in the nineteenth century? The doctrines and ideals of our democracy remained remarkably constant for more than a century after the establishment of the Constitution. A half-dozen European countries exhibited a far greater rate of progress in government for the people and by the people. This stability would have pleased many of the Fathers of the Republic. It would have been a happy surprise to them as well, for they feared that the prophecies of the Old World critics would materialize and that liberty would run into license and license be cured only by dictatorship. But the ship of state veered little from the course charted by the first pilots.

The accepted explanation is that the Constitution was drawn up by the propertied class for the sake of the propertied class and that since 1789 capital has used every means in its possession to preserve its ancient privileges. That this system has not produced fascistic results is due largely to the fact that land and resources were abundant and property was widely distributed. There is little to question in this view. America has been a nation of small capitalists and they have maintained a form of government that served well the interests of that class.

It is among the noncapitalists that opposition might have been expected. Laborers, miners, farm tenants and hired hands could have put an army of voters in the field to challenge the supremacy of their opponents. Had such an army been mustered, the commands would have been issued in every language of Europe, for foreign-born citizens would have constituted the majority. The ignorance and apathy of immigrants and their herding to the polls by employers have been cited as reasons for the failure of such a party to coalesce; but this explanation leaves out of account a more fundamental consideration.

The naturalized voter might be without funds or land, he might inhabit a slum tenement, but no matter how miserable his surroundings he was a capitalist at heart. The hope that brought him across the Atlantic did not fail him; and the possession by others of wealth and leisure spurred him on to secure the same advantages for himself and his children. It would seem, therefore, that the constant influx of such persons for more than a century provided American democracy with a great stabilizing force.

A consideration of some of the factors productive of liberalism in American history will illuminate this point. Liberal and even radical movements mark every stage of our national development. There were men in the ranks during the Revolutionary War who expressed ideas that caused the leaders to tremble. The assault upon property in Shays's Rebellion in 1786 was one of the forces that consolidated the movement for the Federal Constitution. The 1830's and 1840's teemed with reform proposals and utopias; and again in the 1880's and 1890's the trumpets of radical reform echoed throughout the land. Any classification of American messiahs is impossible, but one characteristic they had in common. Nearly all of those who commanded any appreciable following derived from the old stock of the colonies and were two or three hundred years removed from their pioneer and immigrant ancestors.

The American radicalism of the nineteenth century assumed two distinct forms. From 1830 to 1850 it was a reflection of the contemporary European scene. From

1880 to 1900 it was an attempt to preserve the American individualism then threatened by a growing monopoly in land and industry. At no time was Europe more alive with schemes of social betterment than in the second third of the century. Industrialization had bred problems that existing governmental arrangements could not solve; and, as is usual in such circumstances, there were those who said, "Scrap the whole machine and begin anew." Robert Owen in England and Fourier in France drew up their respective plans; and the printing press spread their ideas throughout the literate world. In the United States, where an ardent humanitarianism had taken over the ethical impulses of the stern theology of the forefathers, these systems were adopted as a program of action. Europe invented, but America experimented. A handful of Owen's communities and two score of Fourier's phalanxes were organized to make the New World really new, but they all died a natural death. The second period, that beginning in the 1880's, was more distinctively a native product. While European reformers were finding a remedy in socializing the state, Americans were engaged in agitating for a return to first principles. Their program was, in part, a reaction to the regimentation of the Civil War; in part, also, it was a longing for the old freedom of the frontier. The pioneer had met his difficulties, not with the laws and the paternalism of a benevolent government, but with his own initiative and resources. In its extreme form, this doctrine of a régime of no government bore the name of anarchism.

Immigrant reaction in each of these periods confirms the thesis of conservatism. Relatively few of those who came in the twenty years following 1830 exhibited any interest in the experimental communities. That people should live together and attain personal security by losing their individuality in a group was to them no new plan of salvation, no matter how novel it seemed to Americans. Their eighteenth-century immigrant predecessors had formed many religious societies that practiced communism in varying degrees, and no one who knew rural Pennsylvania would say that the communized brethren were more prosperous or happy than the independent German or Scotch-Irish settlers who surrounded them. One principle dominated the immigrants' thinking: their belief in individualism, their conviction that only he who was free to seek opportunity, when and where it beckoned, could make good. Hence, in most instances, the proposals of the reformers were waved aside as fantasies.

Fifty years later, when the atmosphere was again charged with unrest, the bulk of naturalized citizens had the chance once more to declare their position. To be sure, the most radical doctrine of the day, that of anarchism, was introduced into America by German immigrants. Few in number, they attached themselves to the growing labor movement, serving as organizers and editors. In the mushroom city of Chicago, the capital of a labor world that included railroad gangs, miners in the new coal fields, lumberjacks of the northern forests and stevedores of the Great Lakes, these agitators found their best opportunity. As a result of their exertions, the workingmen's papers, led by the *Arbeiter Zeitung* of Chicago, took on the red color of Continental anarchism and preached reform by violence against those in authority. The leaders resolved that during 1886 they would bring to the cause of labor a decisive victory. The disorders reached their climax on the evening of May 5, when strikers were holding a meeting at Haymarket Square in Chicago.[1] More than a hundred police were on duty to preserve the peace. The meeting proved rather dull and tiresome; but as the crowd was beginning to leave, from somewhere and by someone a bomb was thrown. It exploded in the midst of the ranks of the police, killing several and mortally wounding others.

Official zeal demanded that someone pay the penalty. Not knowing whose hands had actually committed the deed, the prosecution turned upon those who had preached violence of this very nature. The *Arbeiter Zeitung* had long urged the use of dynamite against those in authority. It had even instructed its readers how a piece of gas pipe packed with nitroglycerine might be put to service. One of the editors was accustomed to take a group of young men on Sundays across Lake Michigan to the sand dunes of Indiana, where they would spend the day throwing bombs at imaginary capitalists. Since the fragments of iron picked up in Haymarket Square indicated that the death machine had been constructed according to the newspaper's specifications, the editors and those associated

[1] Henry David, *The History of the Haymarket Affair* (N. Y. 1936).

with them were brought to trial, condemned and executed.

The incident is of vital importance in the history of immigration. Since five of the six condemned men were of foreign birth, this fact would seem to disprove the contention that immigrants played a conservative rôle in American society. But a further consideration of the episode belies such a conclusion. In the first place, these men were not typical immigrants. They were exiled revolutionists who had no interest in America other than the changes they could effect in its economic system. In the second place, the millions of their fellow Europeans in the United States left no doubt as to where they stood on the issue of law and order. The immigrant press took prompt occasion to make clear that it desired no change, through violence or otherwise, in the existing system. The writers declared that the constitutional régime of liberty under law was just to all, rich and poor, native and foreigner, and that the absence of any government would only prepare the way for despotism. As further evidence of their attitude, mass meetings of Germans and Scandinavians condemned the traitors, who had cast an ill-deserved repute on all foreign-born, and affirmed their faith in things as they were. Immigrant church conventions also adopted solemn resolutions pledging loyalty to American ideals and approving the process which had brought the offenders to justice.

The history of the next twenty-five years proves that such sentiments represented the general view. In the growing labor movement immigrants exerted, for the most part, a moderating influence. An English cigar maker, Samuel Gompers, was president of the American Federation of Labor almost uninterruptedly from 1886 until his death in 1924. For forty years his cautious and conservative leadership kept the labor movement free from violence and radicalism and stifled all attempts to create an effective proletarian party. Later leaders in the labor movement considered him little less than a renegade to the class he represented and accused him of truckling to the industrial magnates. His reëlection to office year after year was due largely to the support of trade organizations in which immigrant membership was strong.

During the last decade of the century the spirit of political reform took shape in a crusade under the aegis of the People's party. The Populists were overwhelmingly native American in blood. The party arose simultaneously in the South and in the Middle West. In the former region its American character may be assumed because of the fewness of the foreign-born residents. In the West, however, the states in which Populism won its greatest victories were those into which immigrants had been pouring since the close of the Civil War. They constituted a political element which time and again had turned the scale in elections. Few successes had been achieved by any person or cause without their support. But the history of the People's party provides an exception, for the Germans and Scandinavians who had congregated in Iowa, Kansas, Nebraska and the Dakotas cast their votes largely against Populist candidates despite the efforts of orators and newspaper editors to gain their adherence.

This aversion was due partly to their customary conservatism and partly to the influence of the immigrant church. No matter how much the ministers of the various denominations differed in theology, they raised an almost unanimous voice against the Populists and their political heresies. Clerical conservatism could not view with favor any movement which threatened to surround religion with a social life in which unconventional ideas were dominant. The clergy may not have feared the popular election of Senators, free silver or any other particular proposal; but they knew that political radicalism is apt to attract camp followers whose ultimate aim is a new order in religion, morals and family institutions. European clergymen accustomed to the stabilizing influence of a state church thought that American society was already too much secularized. Hence they could not remain neutral in a struggle which might open the door to fresh evils. It is not surprising that the new party met with a noticeable immigrant opposition. Whatever may be true of later agrarian movements, Populism did not stem from the European invasion of the nineteenth century.

In the national legislative battles of the thirty years after 1890 those few Senators who were of foreign birth aligned themselves on the conservative side. An example is the Norwegian-born Senator Knute Nelson of Minnesota, who for thirty years voted consistently with the old-guard Republicans. Every time he sought reëlection he commanded the almost unanimous support of the Scandinavians of his state.

On few occasions did the rank and file of voters have the opportunity of revealing their wishes with regard to a proposed policy by a direct *yes* or *no*. Generally such referenda concerned technical improvements in the machinery of government and, accordingly, they indicate little as to progressive or conservative sentiment. On the question of woman suffrage, however, these fundamental attitudes came into play. When the citizen marked the ballot, he usually expressed his prejudices instead of a reasoned judgment. How immigrants voted is well known. The reminiscences and reports of the suffrage missionaries agree that their opposition was perhaps the most formidable obstacle to overcome. The notion that "Woman's place is in the home" fitted in with every ideal that the peasant had brought with him from Europe; and again the clergy rallied to the support of custom. Wyoming, the first state to extend the presidential franchise to women, was almost one-hundred-per-cent native American at the time of the adoption.

The turn toward liberalism usually came when the first generation of American-born reached adult years. During the governorship of the elder Robert M. La Follette, Wisconsin adopted many governmental innovations — a mild form of state socialism which became known as the "Wisconsin idea." In putting through his program,

IMMIGRATION AND DEMOCRACY 93

Governor La Follette, knowing the traditional reaction to be expected from citizens of alien birth, skillfully sought to win the support of each nationality. He was surprised at the readiness with which the Germans, Scandinavians and Bohemians rallied to his cause; they became, in fact, the bulwark of his party. The reason lay not so much in the governor's persuasiveness as in the change of mental climate that had taken place in the regions still known as "foreign settlements." The Germans were no longer of German birth. The same was true of other groups. The second generation had come upon the scene with its own outlook and reactions.

The appearance of the second generation has always marked a new chapter in the history of any immigrant stock. The Norwegian father considered his children Norwegians; the children considered themselves Americans. In reality they were neither. They were experiencing a transition stage characterized by an exaggerated Americanism which obscured the cultural values they had imbibed from their immigrant surroundings. With the point of view of the older generation the younger had no sympathy; and upon reaching maturity the son hastened to throw off every distinctive feature that had set the father apart from his American neighbors. "Old fashioned" was the inclusive charge directed against the parents — old fashioned in speech, in dress, in methods of work and in standards of conduct. Very often the same judgment was pronounced against the father's political alignment, with the result that the cause of liberalism was strengthened by a wholesale desertion of second-generation voters.

That conservative fathers should have less conservative sons is a phenomenon not unknown in the most stable of countries. Occasionally a rising generation moves *en masse* toward the left. It is doubtful, however, whether such a shift ever before occurred on so large a scale as in recent times in the upper Mississippi Valley. The formation of the Farmers' Nonpartisan League in 1915 was an invitation to both Republicans and Democrats to discard their outworn political programs and make a more fundamental attack upon the difficulties that beset agriculturists. In time the Nonpartisan League of North Dakota expanded into the Farmer-Labor party of the Northwest. Its program grew more revolutionary as it attempted to cope with the larger economic situation under such leaders as Floyd B. Olson, the second-generation Norwegian who occupied the governor's chair in Minnesota.

The domain of contemporary agrarian unrest corresponds closely with the limits within which the millions of immigrants of the years between 1870 and 1900 settled. One need not maintain that this ferment is merely the expression of second-generation radicalism. War-time speculation created many artificial financial burdens for the farmers, and the Great Depression beginning in 1929 rendered their plight desperate. But sixty or even forty years ago the immigrants in this very region lived through times that were relatively just as hard, yet they shunned the political panaceas of their day. Now, having lost the conservatism of new property holders, they join their fellow native Americans in urging governmental measures directed against that aspect of the economic system which their foreign-born fathers had considered its greatest asset: unrestricted free enterprise.

Those Europeans who became urban wage-earners after 1900 found themselves in surroundings so different, and faced prospects so unpromising, that they often united with the Socialist movement. But their proportion to the total has been small despite the fact that many of them had been Socialists in the country of their birth. Probably more immigrant Socialists were lost to the cause in the United States than were won from the ranks of the newcomers. Those who did not join the Republican party as the protector of the industries that employed them, found a home in the more liberal atmosphere of the Democratic party. Neither group, of course, questioned the fundamentals of capitalism. So in this respect also the voters of immigrant stock threw their weight into the scales for conservative progress.

The bulk of naturalized voters in the nineteenth century never grasped the fine points involved in public policy; but they comprehended the basic character of American democracy and usually made its maintenance without essential change their principal political objective. Like a sea that tempers the heat and cold of the surrounding land, the ocean of immigrants moderated the cold of political reaction and the heat of democratic reform. If this interpretation is correct, American democracy of the future will assume a different aspect now that immigration has come to an end. No longer will the laboring class consist predominantly of newcomers who feel they are merely serving an apprenticeship. The workers will use their political power to obtain ever greater economic and social rights, and the politics and democracy of America will more nearly resemble those of Western Europe before the second World War.

V

IMMIGRATION AND PURITANISM

A STRANGE and undefined authority pervades American social and intellectual life, and occasionally its influence extends into the realm of politics. This sovereign force bears the name Puritanism. It has no definition and every person gives it his own meaning. Whenever a patriot honors great men and mighty deeds, he says they were inspired by Puritanism. Whenever a critic of society or art bemoans the dullness and uniformity of the national scene, he traces them back to the blighting effects of Puritanism. Any sort of restraint established by the government or decreed by custom is Puritanism. Any intolerance in the world of ideas is Puritanism. A human prejudice, a stern injustice, an annoying regulation — all derive from the same source. And when occasionally a robust pioneer society breaks all the bounds of propriety and runs into license, the evildoers are personally excused on the plea that this was merely a reaction to Puritanism.

The scholars whose field is literature have had more to say about Puritanism than the theologians and the historians. That perhaps accounts in large part for the vogue of the interpretation. In New England literary culture attained its earliest and fullest development. The figures that loom largest in the history of fiction, poetry and popular philosophy are New England men who flourished when Boston was the intellectual capital of the United States. For better or for worse, historians of literature have recently adopted the policy of interpreting authors and their works in terms of social environment. A poem is no longer the outpouring of an individual's despair or aspirations, and fiction is no longer the imagination having an exciting time. The author must be considered an unconscious scribe jotting down whatever his neighbors and their foibles dictated. Emerson, Longfellow, Hawthorne and Lowell are not individuals. They are Puritan essayists, poets or novelists; and American literature, taking them as models, has been thoroughly artificial because certain standards as to what was fit to print have narrowed the range of emotions that a writer dared to depict.

Until lately most of the critical work in American church history has come from the pens of investigators who started their labors in an iconoclastic mood. The breaking of images has proceeded with such vigor that now the popular heroes and heroines of New England are colorful characters who suffered persecution at the hands of the Puritan divines. American religion, according to this view, started out with an emphasis upon things that were trivial and things that were seen. Outward appearances were the test of piety. Accordingly, hypocrisy was bred into the moral nature and pettiness took the place of that broad sympathy for human weaknesses which should be the basis of all religion. Occasionally, when the contrast between the inside and the outside of the cup became too scandalous, some revivalist would wash it out with a flood of emotionalism. Then excitement would take the place of reason, and finally there would come a reaction and a lethargy that encouraged an even greater contradiction between profession and deed.

Custom has reserved for the historian the sphere of politics, but in recent times he also has widened his interests to cover the broad background of man's varied activities. It is no longer enough to know what happened. One must know why; and the more subtle and personal a factor is, the more weight it can claim as a determining force. Consequently, Puritanism has appeared as an explanation in the most unexpected places. The reform campaigns that periodically overturn municipal administrations are presented, not as a plain revolt of civic decency, but as a sudden reawakening of the primitive American conscience. Candidates for office must expect traits of character that have absolutely no bearing upon official fitness to be exposed to public view. In the past, at least, clergymen have exercised a remarkable influence in determining the availability of men who desired political preferment, and the "Methodist vote" and the "Baptist vote" have been angled for as consistently as the vote of the farmers or laborers. There are some who consider the abolitionist phase of the antislavery movement a nineteenth-century manifestation of the Puritan spirit. By this reasoning the Civil War was only an episode in the history of that cult.

The term Puritanism has also been applied to public policies which have sometimes been expressed in state and federal legislation. What this means is well known: the censorship of literature by a customs inspector; the censorship of the theater by a policeman temporarily taken off his regular beat; the interpretation of what is art and what is indecency by a judge who knows nothing about the canons of culture. In the same category fall the state laws and city ordinances that have laid down precise rules as to how the Sabbath is to be kept holy and, finally, the legal code adopted to preserve temperance, ending in the temporary prohibition amendment to the Constitution. This is what the average citizen refers to as Puritanism: a program that seeks to regulate morals by preventive legislation. Such an attempt has not been unknown in other countries, but in the United States it has been more persistent and more drastic. Out of it have come many of the predominant features of American social life.

So obvious has this national distinction been that the popular mind possesses a standard explanation of its origin and development. It runs about as follows. The most successful colonizers of the North American continent were English Puritans who left the decadent society of the homeland to plant a Bible commonwealth beyond the sea. Permeated through and through by Calvin's theology, they found in the Old Testament the spirit of their government and the text of many of their laws. To preserve this ideal state, they did not hesitate to hang Quakers and drive dissenters into the wilderness; and their sons and daughters were reared in an ecclesiastical atmosphere as harsh as New England's climate. Time softened somewhat the administration of these ideals, but the spirit remained. From its home in the Northeastern states Puritanism was introduced to the West and Southwest by migrating settlers, and the wealth that the merchants accumulated was devoted to the establishment of colleges. From these institutions came one generation of ministers after the other, who gradually captured control of most of the Protestant churches and stamped their teachings upon the pattern of village and country life. The Civil War (which in many ways was an attempt of the South to escape this domination) was a great victory for the ministers and, elated by success, they persisted in their efforts until at last morality was written into the fundamental law of the land in the Eighteenth Amendment.

But who were the Puritans of New England? Much learning has failed to yield satisfactory answers to questions regarding their education, material possessions and practical motives in seeking new homes. Perhaps they were fanatics. On the other hand, they may have been ordinary individuals who, not being deeply concerned with religion, left discipline to the leaders. But whatever they were in spiritual matters, in temporal affairs they were colonists, settlers who were obliged to devote most of their time, thought and energy to chopping down forests, building homes and planting and reaping harvests. They were immigrants, and most of their policies must have been typical immigrant reactions. Whether the European crossed the Atlantic in 1630, 1730 or 1830, the all-absorbing problem that faced him was that of getting settled, with the result that his social life in all of its aspects was colored by the needs of his pioneer status. In a group of settlers these individual needs, multiplied many times over, inevitably became an essential part of community policy.

If a student will investigate the experiences of the millions of nineteenth-century immigrants, saturate himself in their problems, and then study the original records of seventeenth-century Massachusetts without the assistance of any traditional interpretations, he will be amazed to note how familiar the passages sound. Nearly every one of the later immigrant settlements was troubled by its Roger Williams and its Anne Hutchinson, who had to be cast out for the sake of religious peace. Nearly every group had its statesmen who made sacrifices to build a college lest the people be left to an illiterate ministry. Each had its fanatics in social philosophy and religious practice, and Puritanism was the spirit that permeated all. So striking is the parallel that one hesitates to doubt that the Germans, Swedes, Finns and all the rest of them would have been just as intolerant in their laws if they had possessed the same legal rights of self-government as the Fathers of New England. The vocabulary of Calvin may have provided the phrases in which the ideals were expressed, but those ideals were an outgrowth of the necessities of daily life.

The *Journal* of John Winthrop, many times governor of Massachusetts Bay, provides an enlightening passage which may be taken as a starting point. Winthrop is remembered as one of the milder and more humane of the Fathers and the régime of which he was a part never had his complete approbation. But crime and disorder appeared in a startling degree among the settlers. The authorities, obliged to take action, disputed as to how severe the action should be. The ministers went into conference, and the passage continues, "The next morning they delivered their several reasons, which all sorted to this conclusion, that strict discipline both in criminal offences and in martial affairs, was more needful in plantations than in a settled state, as tending to the honor and safety of the gospel."[1] To repeat the significant words: "strict discipline ... more needful in plantations than in a settled state." This is the clue to immigrant Puritanism.

Why a stricter discipline? In the Old World a person was likely to lead a respectable life because of the restraints of family and tradition. But in the New World these restraints were gone. No one knew him; life was harder; and the former pleasures were not available. Moral standards had been an outward prop, not an inner support, and now the prop was gone. Law had to do for the individual what he could not do for himself; and law did it, not primarily for the individual's good but for the protection

[1] John Winthrop, *History of New England from 1630 to 1649* (Boston, 1853), I, 212.

of society. Every frontier lived through its period of lawlessness before government caught up; and when the miners of California formed vigilance committees and hanged horse thieves and claim jumpers, they were merely being puritanical in their own way. The famous Blue Laws are also understandable: no person to smoke more than two pipes a week because the few acres already cleared must be planted with wheat, not tobacco, or starvation might result; no cooking on Sunday because during the long hours when the family was in church the embers might flare up and put the whole settlement ablaze; no loitering or fishing in the woods on the part of the young men because the Indians might fall upon them, seize their rifles, and have the settlers at their mercy. Thus one can page through the code and reason out a practical, everyday explanation of the regulations that now seem so strange.

Occasionally a reader chances upon one of the intimate diaries in which a Puritan recorded the duties and pastimes of his fleeting hours. Before many paragraphs are covered there comes the inevitable exclamation: "But these saints weren't so puritanical after all." There were picnics and dinner parties and courtships and ordinations — especially ordinations. The bill for refreshments (port, sherry and also the harder varieties) amounted to a total that certainly would have cared for all the poor of the parish for many years. When a church was dedicated, when the ministers gathered in annual conference, when the judges met in conclave, few restrictions or inhibitions were evident.[2] All this illustrates what may be called the practical aspect of Puritanism. Regulations were adopted not so much for the moral good of those who did the regulating, as because there were many in the community who could not be trusted to restrain themselves. The first temperance society in America was founded in 1789 by the farmers of Litchfield County, Connecticut; but note that they pledged not only to abstain themselves, but also to refuse their hired hands any liquor as part of their rations. That was the essence of practical Puritanism — the restriction of others.[3]

New England Puritanism had its ups and downs. As the influx of colonists ceased and life became more settled, the early régime relaxed, only to revive in a more bitter and unnatural form whenever some danger loomed. Shortly before 1700, war with France and the threat of invasion led to a Puritan outburst which sought to free the land of all the evil spirits that had lodged in the mortal frames of old women.[4] In the 1740's there was again war with France, and every frontier community lived in terror of Indian massacre. Again the ministers could preach the need of reformation, and the Great Awakening sought to restore the piety of earlier days. But when the emerg-

[2] The drinking habits of the New England clergy are illustrated by F. O. Erb, *The Development of the Young People's Movement* (Chicago, 1917), 3-5.

[3] This pledge is printed in Daniel Dorchester, *The Liquor Problem in All Ages* (N. Y., 1884), 166.

[4] G. L. Kittredge, *Witchcraft in Old and New England* (Cambridge, 1928), 371-372; R. M. Bayles, *History of Windham County, Connecticut* (N. Y., 1889), 42.

ency had passed and the evangelizing zeal had cooled, sinners could continue along the broad way in peace.

After the expulsion of the French from North America and the achievement of independence New England reached social maturity. Puritanism was still the tradition that provided the ideal for many of the forms of life, but officials and public opinion condoned scenes and standards that gave the age an aspect of unrestrained license. There was religious indifference. The Sabbath was desecrated. Business morals were low and Yankee traders bore an unsavory name in most of the ports of the seven seas. Drunkenness was a prevailing vice.[5] John Harriott, whose *Struggles through Life* presents a varied picture of a seaman's career in the latter days of the eighteenth century, found in Boston "more private debauchery than I ever knew in any other part of the world."[6] Contemporary moralists blamed the condition on the laxness attending the war of the Revolution; others ascribed it to the vogue of French philosophy and infidelity. Is it not more reasonable to suppose that the conditions that had nourished Puritanism had disappeared and the Puritan Age had run its course?

A more pleasing aspect of the change was the liberalism that appeared in intellectual circles. A theater was opened

---

[5] *History of Middlesex County, Connecticut* (N. Y., 1884), 272. One of the early nineteenth-century German writers on America warned emigrants that the evil effects of the Revolution were still noticeable. E. L. Brauns, *Praktische Belehrungen und Rathschläge für Reisende und Auswanderer nach Amerika* (Brunswick, 1829), 226.

[6] John Harriott, *Struggles through Life* (London, 1808), 36.

in Boston and (what would probably have shocked the ancestors more) a Catholic chapel was erected. Tolerance of opinions and practices was the mark of a gentleman. The pioneer Catholic clergy of New England were elected to learned and select societies, and Protestants flocked to the services to hear the creed of the Church expounded.[7] Puritan doctrine was softened into Unitarianism and Unitarianism was further softened into Universalism. Many gave up all religion and became humanitarians of the literary variety. For over a generation this spirit reigned and, finally, in the 1830's and 1840's it blossomed out into the so-called "golden age" of New England — a period of literature and philosophy when the writings of Continental scholars received a welcome in the universities and their theories were eagerly absorbed by the clergymen who no longer found satisfaction in the spiritual food of their fathers.

Perhaps it was too good to last. New England was destined to be something other than an agricultural commonwealth. Nature had provided power, and two centuries of industry and parsimony had produced an accumulation of capital. In the years that followed the War of 1812 commercial ports and rural villages were industrialized. Local capitalists constructed cotton and woolen mills, and many a country girl spent a few months or a year or two tending the spindles until she earned a

---

[7] The tolerance of the educated New Englanders is commented upon in the *Jesuit* (Boston), March 19 and July 23, 1831; and in the *United States Catholic Intelligencer* (Boston), Sept. 21, 1832.

dowry. But there was other labor to be done — heavy, dirty work that no New Englander would perform for the pittance offered: canals to be dug, foundations to be laid, dams to be constructed. And so the Irishman came.

In no other part of the United States at the time would the Irishman have felt himself more of a stranger and received less of a welcome. Two hundred years before, twenty thousand Englishmen had founded the Puritan colonies. Since that first influx the current of immigration had largely passed them by. A few hundred families from Ulster had come shortly after 1700, but their descendants could not be counted upon to extend a cordial greeting to the Catholic Hibernians. Nevertheless, no hardship could daunt them, no ridicule discourage their persistence. The son sent for his father and the father for his wife and children. They crowded together in the garrets of the cities and built "shanty towns" wherever a vacant lot and discarded boxes and timbers could be discovered.

No matter how sympathetic one might feel toward these new colonists, he could not overlook the practical problems created by their presence. Penniless, hungry and often sick, the immigrant's first acquaintance in the community was the officer whose duty it was to relieve the poor. Even when employment was obtained, the Irishman remitted such a large percentage of his small wage to his native land that poverty and squalor seemed to be his perpetual state. In the eyes of his American neighbors he was the representative of a thriftless and improvident race whose coming threatened to destroy the standards of living and the aspect of comfort that had previously prevailed.

Honest poverty the Yankee might have condoned, but this unfortunate state, he believed, was the result not of divine affliction but of the devil drink. The immigrant gulped American whisky and found it excellent in taste and effective in results. Not the least of its virtues was its price. In a letter in which he described the advantages of the New World, one immigrant wrote, "Give my very kind love to Father, and tell him if he was here he could soon kill himself by drinking if he thought proper. ... I can go into a store, and have as much brandy as I like to drink for three half-pence, and all other spirits in proportion."[8] This advantage the newcomers did not hesitate to make the most of. The fatigue of heavy labor demanded a stimulant; fever and ague required an antidote; homesickness had to be dispelled. For all these ailments whisky provided a universal remedy. It was, however, a remedy that was taken socially and produced the reckless conviviality that expatriates always inspire in one another when they meet over the cup in a foreign clime. Pay day was Saturday night, which Puritan custom considered part of the Sabbath; and on that evening shouts

[8] G. P. Scrope, ed., *Extracts of Letters from Poor Persons Who Emigrated Last Year to Canada and the United States* (London, 1831), 23. Warnings regarding the disasters that followed cheap liquor are numerous in all immigrant literature. See, for example, S. H. Collins, *The Emigrant's Guide to and Description of the United States of America* (Hull, 1830), 87, 111-112.

of happiness and sounds of strife arose from the hovels and streets of shanty town.[9] The Yankee drunkard was of the Rip Van Winkle type, an easy-going, humorous village character, the friend of children and dogs. He became more and more stupefied and finally reached a fitting end. Immigrant drunkenness, on the other hand, was violent, and as dangerous to innocent bystanders as to the circle of drinkers. Catholic priests who followed their parishioners to the labor camps fought against intemperance as the supreme immigrant vice. Their warnings and sermons are source materials as vivid as any of the complaints of the outraged Congregational clergy.[10]

At first, the only official measures were directed against the burden of poverty. Every incoming foreign passenger was forced to pay a head tax, and from the fund thus accumulated the towns were reimbursed for any expenses incurred.[11] The social difficulties were neglected on the theory that American institutions would cure anything. In the meantime the immigrants established their own institutions; and by 1850 New England was the home of two peoples, each of whom possessed its own manner of living, its own standards of conduct and an intense hostility toward the other. With the large invasion of hungry

[9] Such disturbances, during the course of one year, are reported in the *Boston Courier*, Jan. 19, April 8, 11, June 20, Aug. 3, Sept. 5, 12, 1848.

[10] *Catholic Herald* (Phila.), Nov. 5, 1840; *United States Catholic Intelligencer*, Feb. 17, 1832; *Boston Pilot*, Sept. 1, 1838, July 24, 1841.

[11] The shortcomings of this system as it operated in Massachusetts are explained in the "Report on Foreign Paupers," *Massachusetts House Documents for 1835*, no. 60.

Irishmen in 1847 and thereafter, the natives arose in revolt. Economic jealousy, religious bigotry and social disapproval prompted the formation of secret societies collectively designated in history the Know-Nothing movement.[12] Politically, the movement sought to restrict immigration and hinder naturalization. Unofficially, it aimed to curb the growth of the Catholic Church. But socially it became a part of a revival of Puritanism, and it was one of the strongest factors leading to that revival.

Attention has earlier been drawn to a distinctive feature of Puritanism: the regulation of the morals and actions of those whom the regulators deemed dangerous to society because they were unable to take care of themselves. Here was a situation that encouraged a reapplication of this principle, and the statute books of every New England state record the results.[13] In 1851 Maine adopted a state-wide law prohibiting the manufacture and sale of intoxicants. During the next five years practically every Northern state battled over similar proposals and many of them borrowed the "Maine Law" as a weapon against intemperance. Prohibition, it is true, was not an official plank of the Know Nothings; but the device appealed to

[12] This antagonism is reflected in the reports of the city missionaries whose attitude had hitherto been distinctly tolerant. Executive Committee of the Benevolent Fraternity of Churches, *Seventeenth Annual Report* (1851), 21–24, and *Eighteenth Annual Report* (1852), 24.

[13] G. H. Haynes, "A Know Nothing Legislature," Am. Hist. Assoc., *Annual Report for 1896*, I, 177–187; "The Doings of the Last Connecticut Legislature on Temperance and Liberty," *New Englander*, XII (1854), 449–456.

the more moderate and practical element. As a writer in the *New Englander* pointed out, persecution of aliens will do no good; ostracism cannot change their habits. "Beget about them a pure moral atmosphere," he wrote, "so they and their children will grow up strong in the virtues that constitute a good citizen." [14]

Both the temperance agitation and the Know-Nothing movement produced an inevitable reaction; but the spirit of Puritanism was again breathed into the life of the churches. When many of the states repealed the prohibitory laws, the clergymen and their faithful cohorts were not discouraged. A return to state-enforced prohibition remained a constant hope. An impetus was given by the hard times that followed the Panic of 1857. Moralists pointed to the hardships and suffering that immigrant families in particular endured, and blamed the difficulties upon the improvidence of the drinking father. The despair also strengthened religious zeal, and the outburst of enthusiasm known as the Revival of 1858 stamped the reborn Puritanism upon a rising generation of ministers and people. For the time being, the full effects could not be seen because the antislavery crusade obscured everything but the status of the Negro. But after the Civil War the churches returned to the earlier conflict and inaugurated a new era of reform, with the nation instead of the state as the ultimate object of their endeavors.

In this new offensive the churches which had been

[14] "Immigration; Its Evils and Their Remedies," *New Englander*, XIII (1855), 262-276.

puritanized by the New England influence were aided by allies who came from a quarter in which little assistance would normally have been expected. The German or Scandinavian who set out to establish a home in a pioneer agricultural region obviously found himself in an environment different from that which surrounded the New England Irishman. Out on the prairie or deep in the forest American institutions were often entirely lacking or, if present, they were too weak to be effective in enforcing local standards. Many of the settlers were as respectable in conduct as any Eastern deacon, but the tide of migration had carried in a class of native Americans who rejoiced in the freedom of the West and disported themselves riotously in the crossroads taverns.[15] It was with this social class that the immigrant from abroad was generally thrown. Here was American liberty with a vengeance, and he proceeded to cast off all the restraints that European society had bred in him. As elsewhere, homesickness and dreary labor were incentives to conviviality, and the comradeship offered by the native rowdies was eagerly accepted. The physical and social mortality among people unaccustomed to such ways of living was high. In a large number of cases immigration, instead of being a step upward, was a plunge downward. As successive groups of any nationality arrived, the young men among them accepted the company and adopted the standards of their predecessors. The history of nearly

[15] See, for example, *Home Missionary and American Pastor's Journal* (N. Y.), I (1828–1829), 10, 29, 48, 88, 167–168.

every immigrant settlement reveals that at some time it passed through this stage of drunkenness and revelry.[16]

When the first clergyman of the faith that these foreigners had professed at home appeared upon the scene, his work was cut out for him. To baptize and confirm was not so important as to conduct a clean-up campaign. Irrespective of his past inclinations, he was forced to adopt a program of reform and to forbid pastimes and pleasures that the ecclesiastical rules of his early training had condoned. Thus the immigrant church was started upon a career of Puritanism which, at first, had absolutely no connection with the saints at Boston, the fountainhead from which all such American tendencies are supposed to flow.

A distinction must be made, however, between the Roman Catholic Church, a world-wide organization with more than a thousand years of experience in pioneering, and the Protestant denominations suddenly called upon to enter into undertakings for which no machinery existed. This latter group will be considered first. A Continental state church looked with no favor upon emigration. As an organ of the government it often discouraged it. Among the arguments presented to the head of a family who was anxiously considering the step was the danger

---

[16] Fredrika Bremer, *The Homes of the New World* (N. Y., 1853), I, 635. A missionary who visited the Norwegian settlement in Dane County, Wisconsin, in 1850 reported, "Such gross immorality I never witnessed before — it was offensive to come within the sphere poisoned by their breath." *Home Missionary*, XXIII (1850), 120.

involved in bringing up sons and daughters in a country which was described as a spiritual waste.[17] Every letter from across the Atlantic told of the drunkenness and misery in the immigrant settlements. These same letters prompted others to urge that clergymen, supported by church funds, be sent out to bring together the scattered faithful and organize congregations that would restore the moral atmosphere of the homeland. But these requests were refused. Action of this kind, it was stated, would be interpreted as governmental encouragement of emigration. The more hard-hearted officials argued that those who deliberately separated themselves from their native country and its benevolent institutions should suffer the consequences of their folly.[18]

What state churches refused to do was, therefore, undertaken by benevolent individuals. Sometimes it was the enterprise of a single person, sometimes of an association formed for the purpose. Methods which had been evolved for subsidizing missionaries in India and China were now applied for the benefit of benighted emigrants. Among the clergymen, candidates offered themselves for this field as others had volunteered for service in heathen lands; and, as in the latter case, they tended to be men of more

[17] G. J. Malmin, ed., "Bishop Jacob Neumann's Word of Admonition to the Peasants," Norwegian–American Hist. Assoc., *Studies and Records*, I, 95–109.

[18] The attitude of the Prussian government is indicated in a memoir by the Minister for Internal Affairs, dated February 17, 1845, in the Prussian archives at Berlin-Dahlem, under the classification AA III R 1, Auswanderung aus Europa, 11, vol. 1, no. 1458.

zeal, with stricter standards of conduct, than their fellow ministers who remained at home in the comfortable security of an ecclesiastical position as strong as the state. As a result, the immigrant church started out under the leadership of men with a strong bent toward Puritanism.[19]

This inclination was firmly fixed as a permanent trait when the missionary entered upon his duties. Responsibility rested heavily upon the shoulders of the Lutheran or Reformed pastor, who found himself the moral leader in a settlement of fellow countrymen intoxicated with the ideas and the liquor of the Republic. His coming was welcomed by the sober members of the colony. They organized themselves into an ecclesiastical body, sacrificed to build a church, and set out to restore the good name of German, Swede or whatever it might be.

From this endeavor Puritanism received another impetus. To be successful, even among its own constituency, an immigrant institution had to have the good will of the native Americans. But the respectable, middle-class American looked with suspicion upon an organization which was, he thought, a branch of a monarchical government. In his opinion a state church was no church because the individual was born into it. But every American church was a union of believers who deliberately, under no compulsion, chose to belong to it, to contribute to

[19] This tendency is illustrated in the career of the Reverend T. N. Hasselquist, one of the founders of the Swedish Augustana Synod. O. F. Ander, *T. N. Hasselquist: the Career and Influence of a Swedish-American Clergyman, Journalist and Educator* (Rock Island, Ill., 1931), 7.

its support and to pattern their daily life upon the code of morality that it decreed. These American churches undertook to proselyte among the immigrants and they argued that the adopted citizen, along with his new-found glory as a political individual, should also acquire religious individuality.

Accordingly, in self-defense, the immigrant church was forced to adopt standards that conformed to the ideals of the prevailing denominationalism. An incident or two will illustrate the point. It was a hot July Sunday in Madison, Wisconsin, in 1857. Fifty or sixty Scandinavians attended religious services and then rowed across the lake and enjoyed a picnic afternoon and evening — eating, probably drinking, singing and perhaps engaging in country dances. The event was observed by many, but the picnickers were not prepared for the barrage of criticism that appeared in the local paper, warning them to behave like respectable Americans if they wanted to enjoy the privileges of the country. A worse blow followed when their own clergyman sided with the natives and forbade the faithful to repeat the experience. Thereupon a debate ensued in the columns of the Norwegian paper. The revelers asked: since such Sunday pastimes are a common custom in Norway and the clergymen do not condemn but, in fact, partake in them, why does the church forbid in America what is encouraged in Norway? Is not a sin in one place a sin in another? The reply of authority was: we do not argue this on the basis of intrinsic right or wrong; the fact is clear that such practices bring our church into disrepute, and whatever weakens the position of the church is wrong.[20]

The second incident is drawn from the autobiography of one of the immigrant missionaries. He came to the New World at considerable personal sacrifice in order that he might organize the scattered congregations into some uniformity in theology and administration. It was not long before he became aware that his success was being hindered by the rumor that he was a drunkard and Sabbath-breaker. Investigation revealed the origin of these charges. The first was based upon his habit of stopping while on long horseback journeys to refresh himself with a glass of wine at a country tavern. The second was the result of his calling together a congregational meeting on a Sunday afternoon to consider the worldly question of how much salary the church could raise for the support of a settled minister. Being a practical person, he at once "reformed" and determined at the first opportunity to reveal the strictness of his code. The opportunity came. In the ranks of one congregation was a member who had fallen into evil ways. Admonition did no good and he was excluded from the fellowship of the church. This was a procedure which in Europe was reserved for only the most despicable conduct and which rendered the victim almost a social outcast. This stigma the accused one refused to bear and argued that the congregation had no authority so to act. To maintain his point he boldly appeared at the next business session. The minister, who

[20] *Emigranten* (Madison, Wis.), Jan. 20, 1858.

presided, announced that when all strangers had withdrawn they would proceed. No one left. Thereupon the pastor, addressing the offender by name, told him (in proper ecclesiastical language) to get out and stay out. He didn't budge. At once the clergyman descended from his place, seized the sinner by the collar and hurled him through the door. This was not the last of the incident. The preacher was summoned before the nearest justice of the peace, charged with assault and battery, found guilty and fined. In recording the outcome he made no complaint regarding American justice. On the contrary, there is a note of triumph in the account, for never again did anyone in the community say there was no discipline in the Lutheran Church. The conduct of its members was as irreproachable as any Methodist, Baptist or Presbyterian could demand.[21]

This may be described as spontaneous immigrant Puritanism. It was reënforced by a closer association with the American churches. Comparatively little financial support was received from Europe and, when the undenominational American Home Missionary Society offered a struggling pastor a subsidy of a hundred dollars a year, there was no reason for him to refuse. But this society insisted that only earnest souls be tolerated in the membership of the congregation, and, although no definition of "earnestness" was provided, prudent pastors knew that exemplary conduct was considered a

[21] J. W. C. Dietrichson, *Reise blandt de norske emigranter i de forenede nordamerikanske fristater* (Stavanger, 1846), 38, 70.

necessary quality and exercised discipline accordingly.[22] From this beginning the relations with the institutions of the country were expanded. Young men who were educated for the ministry were often sent to a theological seminary in New England and, when the immigrant churches founded colleges to train pastors for their own congregations, those institutions could not escape the forms or the spirit that prevailed at Harvard, Yale and Princeton.

The process of Puritanization can be followed by anyone who studies the records of a congregation or the minutes of a synod. Discipline became more and more strict. One after the other, social pleasures that were brought from the Old World fell under the ban. Temperance and Sunday observance were early enforced; then card playing and dancing were prohibited. Simplicity in dress and manner of living became prime virtues. The children of the immigrants were the object of much concern. When they began to forget the language of their parents and absorb the culture of their American contemporaries, an effort was made to prevent their mingling in surrounding society by decreeing the sinfulness of any pastime that tempted such association. By the last quarter of the nineteenth century the Protestant immigrant churches had adopted so much of the "New England atmosphere" that clergymen who came from the Euro-

---

[22] See the letter of Reverend T. N. Hasselquist to the Home Missionary Society, dated Galesburg, Illinois, February 3, 1854. Gunnar Westin, ed., *Emigranterne och kyrkan* (Stockholm, 1932), 70–73.

pean seminaries of the various denominations were strangers in theology and ecclesiastical practice.[23]

That part of the Irish immigration which settled in the West and the large number of Germans who were of the Catholic faith were subjected to a régime mild in comparison with that of their Protestant neighbors. When the settlers arrived upon the scene, the Catholic Church was already present. Over a century before, missions had been established among the Indians and the flexible framework of the Church was ready to expand as soon as the need for another kind of service was apparent. When the immigrants arrived priests were not far behind. Sometimes they were in the van of the movement, with funds to build a church that would act as a magnet encouraging the newcomers to locate within sight of the steeple. The rapid multiplication of dioceses in the region beyond the mountains testifies to the efficiency of the system.[24] Accordingly, the Church was more concerned with prevention than with cure, and less drastic measures proved necessary. The person who went astray could not

---

[23] Knut Hamsun was surprised to note that the ministers, instead of discussing theology, preached "Boston morals." Knut Hamsun, *Fra det moderne Amerikas aandsliv* (Copenhagen, 1889), 210.

[24] The history of the early colonizing activities of the Catholic clergy has not been written, but there is contemporary information regarding their efforts in the *Boston Pilot*, March 13, 1858; May 7, Aug. 20, 1859; *New York Freeman's Journal*, Sept. 2, 1854; Sept. 25, 1858; *American Celt* (Buffalo), Aug. 18, Sept. 22, Dec. 1, 1855; *Berichte der Leopoldinen Stiftung* (Vienna), XII (1839), 38; XVII (1844), 32. The later activities are described in Sister Mary Evangela Henthorne, *The Irish Catholic Colonization Association of the United States* (Champaign, Ill., 1932).

so universally blame his fall upon the absence of spiritual advisers; once lost, he was lost for good. Those who from the beginning identified themselves with the Church felt at home, and all the restraining influences of their native village were in operation. No new prohibitions were added to the commandments they had known from youth. Moreover, the Catholic Church was less sensitive to the opinion of the Americans. It realized that it was viewed with suspicion; a certain amount of persecution was taken for granted. The oldest institution in western civilization was not going to revise its program because a few Yankees looked upon it with disfavor.

In the growth of that body of restrictive laws and customs called Puritanism, the Catholic Church is usually accounted a retarding force. Never did it enter wholeheartedly into the campaign to make people moral by police regulations. This desirable end could be achieved by other methods.[25] In the course of time, however, the American hierarchy realized that they were dealing with a situation that had no precedent. Not only did many members of their congregations succumb to the prevailing immigrant vice, but some of the most prosperous parishioners were key men in the liquor trade. Who could produce better beer than the brewer from Munich? And he was a Catholic. Who was a more genial and efficient bartender than the Irishman? And he was a stanch supporter of his religion. The American Protestant press

---

[25] "Prohibitory Legislation: Its Cause and Effect," *Catholic World*, XXVII (1879), 182–204.

associated the two facts, and the Church, for the sake of its public honor, had no alternative but to take action.[26]

Organized and encouraged by bishops and priests, a temperance agitation which left unaffected no one in the constituency was set under way. The archbishop of St. Paul, in whose province so many Catholic immigrants had settled, assumed the leadership, and under his direction public opinion was changed. Men connected with the liquor trade were retired from their positions as lay leaders, and all efforts which sought to secure reform by imposing high licenses and restricting hours received church support. The archbishop was frank in declaring that, if improvement were not secured by these measures, he would not hesitate to support the policy of prohibition.[27] This attitude, it is true, was not generally accepted: the majority had faith in the ultimate success of less drastic means. Nevertheless, the Catholic Church, like the other immigrant churches, helped to form that ecclesiastical sentiment which was the largest single element in putting prohibition temporarily in the Federal Constitution.

To complete the picture, it is necessary to consider a third section of the country — the South. If the theory that colonial Puritanism was more practical than theological is sound, then it should have appeared outside New England. It did. In what direction should we look? Sun-

---

[26] John Ireland, "The Catholic Church and the Saloon," *N. Am. Rev.*, CLIX (1894), 498–505.

[27] John Ireland, *The Church and Modern Society* (N. Y., 1897), 287.

day observance? The resident of colonial Virginia who failed to attend the established service on the Sabbath incurred a penalty of fifty pounds of tobacco. The law of New Netherland decreed that not only were ordinary labor, hunting and fishing prohibited on that day, but also "going on pleasure parties in a boat, car, or wagon before, between, or during divine service" — a regulation that covered most contingencies. Or shall we consider orthodoxy? A man might be sentenced to death for blasphemy in Maryland as well as in New Haven.[28] Or is our interest in intolerance? Massachusetts was not the only place where Quakers could expect opposition. In the Virginia records appear items such as, "Quakers whipped," "Quaker fined for entertaining a Quaker," "June 10, 1658, general persecution of Quakers directed." [29]

But south and west of the Hudson the system did not assume a theological aspect, and it did not become an honored tradition. New York remained a colony of two parts: the sleepy valley of the Hudson River, where Dutch farmers smoked peacefully and, if they ever contemplated any excesses, never got around to action; and the city of New York, which was constantly thronged with rowdy sailors — but no one, not even Puritans, ever attempted to reform sailors on shore leave. New Jersey and Pennsylvania possessed a considerable Quaker element; and the

[28] Edward Channing, *History of the United States*, I (N. Y., 1905), 530, 535–536.
[29] Conway Robinson, "Notes from the Council and General Court Records," *Va. Mag. of Hist. and Biog.*, VIII (1900–1901), 166.

largest contingent of early immigrants was made up of German sectarians bound together in communistic societies which were ruled by an authority more severe than any Boston theocracy would presume to decree. The other large immigration was of Presbyterians from Ulster, who brought with them a severe code and a strict discipline.

Below the Mason and Dixon line, however, the evolution is more enlightening. Reference has already been made to legislation in Virginia and Maryland. The statute books of both colonies abound with enactments which, had they appeared in Massachusetts or Connecticut, would have been considered evidences of Puritan bigotry. But the South did not remain puritanical in its society. Laws were allowed to fall into disuse. Virginia in particular became the scene of a civilization which in comfort and tolerance is always taken as the direct antithesis of everything Puritan. The horse-racing parson, the plantation master who loved his mint juleps, the gay gatherings of young and old in the provincial capital at Williamsburg, are evidences of a society beyond the pioneer state. But they are evidences of something else as well. The small farm had been superseded by the large plantation. Economic life revolved around tobacco, and slaves had taken the place of white servants.

In a history of Puritanism in America, slavery deserves a chapter because, from the definition that has been adopted, slavery was Puritanism raised to the nth degree. When the labor class (or it may be designated the lower class) consisted of slaves, no code of moral behavior was necessary. The upper ranks of society curbed the lower, not by state law but by personal decree. Every master established the standards of morality to which his Negroes must submit and he determined the punishment to be meted out in case of infraction. In any matter his will was stronger than the ties of marriage or family, and his decisions were superior to the precepts of religion. Only occasionally did the law interfere between owner and slave and then the presumption was that the former was in the right.

It is not surprising that the South with a social system of this nature did not feel the wave of Puritanism that arose in the 1850's. The Maine Law agitation affected it only slightly. But fifty years later the situation was reversed. Then the Southern states led in the movement for prohibition; and it was evident that a change of far-reaching influence had taken place. That change, of course, flowed from the abolition of slavery. With its disappearance chaos entered into the relations of black and white, rich and poor, pious and wicked. What the immigrant was in the North, the Negro was in the South — a laborer whose daily life and mental attitude encouraged overindulgence in the cup that cheers. Restraint of some sort was necessary and now, in the South as earlier in the North, the state undertook duties of moral supervision.[30]

[30] L. S. Blakey, *The Sale of Liquor in the South* (N. Y., 1912). How the presence of Negroes and "poor whites" fostered the growth of prohibition sentiment is explained in an article by J. E. White, "Prohibition: The New Task and Opportunity of the South," *S. Atl. Quar.*, VII (1908), 130–142.

The movement for temperance gathered force with each decade that followed the Civil War. The annual influx of foreigners increased rapidly, finally passing the million mark. This horde of new inhabitants each year lived through all the temptations and all the disillusionments that had been the lot of their predecessors. The Puritans struggled with a situation which constantly became more difficult. Most of the states experimented with various lesser remedies, but after their failure came a return to the practice of prohibition by state law. In less than a year four Southern states became "dry." In the succeeding period other commonwealths in the North and West followed suit.[31] State prohibition, however, encountered difficulties in enforcement because of the ease of interstate transportation.

Accordingly, the Puritans took their agitation to Congress. Here the representatives of the three elements met: Congressmen from the North, who had inherited the strict principles of New England forefathers; Congressmen from the West, who did not dare oppose the desires of the immigrant churches which had such great control over their constituents; and Congressmen from the South, who desired to make national a policy which both religion and practice championed. By 1913, they had secured a law controlling the interstate shipment of liquor, but this was an enactment which could be repealed by any change in congressional sentiment. So the agitation was continued and finally, when the war gave an added impetus

[31] E. H. Cherrington, *The Anti-Saloon League Year Book for 1909*, 179–180.

to governmental control of life and property, the prohibition amendment was adopted. The Eighteenth Amendment will long be remembered as a social experiment, an experiment which many regard with mixed feelings. But to consider the Puritanism that inspired it the twentieth-century child of seventeenth-century bigotry is the most superficial of views. It was a Puritanism which arose out of nineteenth-century conditions, and in the formation of those conditions the millions of immigrants played a significant part.

VI

IMMIGRATION AND AMERICAN CULTURE

THE emigrants caused difficulties for everyone who was concerned with their transportation. They lost their tickets and their children. They missed the train and boarded the wrong boat. Obsessed with the idea that America was a wilderness, they filled ten or twelve boxes with the appurtenances of civilization: clothing to last a lifetime, family heirlooms and the like. Sometimes they added a wagon or a plow. Like the owners, these belongings had a way of never being found where they were supposed to be. Every emigrant who survived the ordeal ruefully indorsed the advice of the agents and ship captains: travel light! This admonition, though seldom followed, was excellent, for the clothes were not suited to the new land and the tools were not adapted to American conditions. The trouble and expense were incurred for nothing.

But if physical luggage counted for little, every man, woman and child brought with him something else that no student of American society can ignore. No statistics were kept of this valuable importation. Had a contemporary charged himself with the duty of measuring or at least describing it, the task of the social historian would be lighter. Each newcomer carried with him habits of life and belief and intellectual and æsthetic tastes. Planted in the American soil, these inbred attitudes were to grow and bear fruit long after the humble individuals who had introduced them had vanished from the scene.

These elusive qualities were present in varying degrees according to the economic and social station of the emigrant. Every literary traveler who has described a visit to the steerage has recorded his surprise at finding, cheek by jowl with stolid peasants, a clergyman, a physician, an artist or a classical scholar. When they were asked what turn of fate had sent them on so venturesome a journey, the usual response was: "For every position at home there are ten applicants. The churches are full, the schools are full, and the universities are overcrowded. Perhaps in the New World, where material needs have overshadowed the intellectual, I may find a place for my special talent." In this way academic overproduction abroad helped to stock America with ready-made professional men whose more theoretical knowledge supplemented the rough-and-ready skill of the native-born.

If the vessel were freighted with British, the prospects of such emigrants were bright. The history of almost every community includes an account of some Irish or Scotch schoolmaster who between terms mastered the intricacies of American law and eventually rose to wealth and prominence. The English and Scots were numerous in medicine and in institutions of higher learning. By the same token, nearly every religious denomination was well provided with Welsh clergymen.

The German intellectual faced greater hazards. The jurist's knowledge of law counted for little in an American court. The medical man who could not converse with his patients was badly handicapped. American boys never respected a pedagogue who spoke with an accent. Such difficulties, however, largely vanished as several million Germans settled in the cities and wide agricultural districts. A world then appeared not unlike that which had been left behind. But this did not occur until the mid-nineteenth century. Up to that time, the professional man who failed to curse the day he left the fatherland was an exception.

Fully aware of this situation, German intellectuals at home pondered ways and means of curing it. They believed that, if the Germans then going to the United States could be concentrated geographically, all the cultural advantages of the homeland might be preserved. Man power was available; only guidance was needed because even the simplest farmer would prefer to settle in a place where the speech and folkways involved a minimum of novelty. To provide this guidance the professors and their adherents evolved innumerable schemes. To list all these imagined colonies is unnecessary. Some persons proposed to establish a town or city to serve as a cultural center for the surrounding settlers. The bolder spirits talked of peopling one of the American states and, as was entirely possible under the Constitution, adopting German as the official language. Then, when the expected break-up of the Union should take place, this

Teutonic commonwealth could embark on an independent career and make such alliances as it desired with the German Confederation or the Zollverein.

The first step in the fulfillment of any of these dreams was the acquisition of land. But the government of the United States, though possessed of millions of acres, proved unwilling to give a single acre for the purpose. It expressed its opinion in unmistakable terms in the year 1818 when the Irish societies of New York and Philadelphia, burdened with a large number of charitable cases, petitioned Congress for a land grant in the West on which to establish their dependents. Congress refused, agreeing with the report of a special committee that it would be undesirable to concentrate alien peoples geographically.[1] If a grant were made to the Irish, the Germans would be the next, and so on with other nationalities. The result would be a patchwork nation of foreign settlements. Probably no decision in the history of American immigration policy possesses more profound significance. By its terms the immigrant was to enjoy no special privileges to encourage his coming; also he was to suffer no special restrictions. His opportunities were those of the native, nothing more, nothing less.

Accordingly, in the early thirties the Germans knew that whatever they accomplished had to be attained through buying land in the usual way, just as other set-

---

[1] *Niles' Weekly Register*, XIV (1818), 211–215; 15 Cong., 1 sess., *House Doc.*, no. 119; *Annals of Congress*, XXXI (15 Cong., 1 sess.), 1013–1014, 1053–1054.

tlers did. Nevertheless several attempts at colonization were made. Every one of the collective projects failed, however. Usually the promoter was accused by his disappointed followers of misspending the funds intrusted to his care, but the record shows that the members themselves were often at fault. When a group reached America, the individual colonist, bound by the company regulations, felt like a caged bird. Everywhere about him he saw tempting opportunities he desired to grasp; his discomforts he blamed on the retarding association of his companions. Accordingly, sooner or later, the value of the joint undertaking was questioned and the leader gave up in disgust. The cage was open and its prisoners flew in all directions.

As we look back from the perspective of a hundred years, we realize that the enterprises were not the complete failures they then seemed. Though the pooled funds were depleted, the cultural objectives, which had constituted the primary motive, were ultimately furthered. When the company disbanded, the cliques that had been formed within the ranks remained together. Instead of one German community, ten or a dozen resulted, and each became a nucleus about which later incoming thousands clustered. These settlements re-created most of the social institutions they had left behind, thereby establishing a culture which counted for more because it was an act of free will, not an imposition from above.

Use of the mother tongue, for instance, continued to be a necessity. The head of the household in his goings about readily picked up a vocabulary of English phrases, but not so his wife, isolated upon the farm. As a result, the family language did not change. The community pastimes of the old country also tended to linger on since those of the natives seemed strange and crude. In like fashion, American church services, conducted with the informality of frontier sects, did not inspire the reverence which the European considered essential to religion. Nor did the free-school system live up to his expectations. A narrow curriculum, no equipment, poorly prepared teachers — all these bred disillusion, while the atmosphere of equality pervading the classroom begot contempt. A child returning from school on the first day of the term reported that the schoolmaster had addressed the assembled six-year-olds as "ladies and gentlemen." "What a world of pedagogical heresy is not revealed in that one phrase," the father wrote to a non-English paper in a plea that his compatriots band together and establish their own school.

Step by step, the expatriates endeavored to reproduce many of the institutions of the homeland. The resulting product often fell short of the model, for the immigrants were generally peasants and the culture they knew was that of their own class, not that of the royal court or of the university town. If this fact altered its character, it also rendered it more adaptable, making it possible to weave the heritage of the Old World into the pattern of the New.

The evolution that transformed the German communities is usually ascribed to the "Forty-eighters" — the refugees who fled from the reaction following the collapse of the revolutions of that year. As we have seen, these exiles formed only a tiny proportion of the whole number of immigrants; but by experience, enthusiasm and personality they were fitted for leadership. In a divided Germany they had infused new life into the people; now, in a country with an unmuzzled press and no police supervision, they faced a similar task. Their names were familiar to every immigrant who had followed the events in the fatherland; and whether as editors or lecturers, they commanded a ready audience wherever they went. Most of them, however, made a fatal error. Instead of transferring their interest to the New World, they continued to center it upon the Old. Residence in America was merely a temporary exile; and energies they might have devoted to the German cause in the United States were frittered away in fantastic attempts to promote another uprising in the country they still considered home.

For this reason it is easy to overestimate the rôle of the Forty-eighters. Even without their presence a quickening of nationalistic sentiment was due among the German Americans. This is clearly indicated by the fact that, though neither the Irish nor the Scandinavians received any similar additions to their ranks, both groups also experienced a cultural renaissance at this time. The explanation is simple. Communities that had been founded ten or fifteen years before had now reached maturity; the hard days of pioneering were over. Most of the settlers had acquired comfort; some had obtained wealth; a select few, who constituted a sort of immigrant aristocracy, had established standards which all tried to copy. The arrival of two or three million new immigrants during the period merely tended to elevate socially those who had come before.

Moreover, the Know-Nothing movement strengthened nationalistic feeling among the foreign stocks. When the natives combined to crush what they considered the undue influence of alien groups, they committed a tactical error, for the newcomers, far from being crushed, were prompted to consolidate their hitherto scattered forces. In any case, the Know-Nothing attack came too late to be effective. In many parts of the country the naturalized citizens were now so numerous as to wield the balance of power in closely contested elections. The old Democratic and new Republican parties, frightened by the existence of this army of voters, hastened to disavow all connection with the Know Nothings; but the immigrants refused to forget the insults to which they had been subjected and replied to such overtures with an exaggerated Germanism or Irishism. This attitude stemmed partly from offended pride and partly from a realization of the pleasant fact that they had come to occupy so important a place in American life.

By 1860 a vigorous cultural development was under way in every immigrant group. Much of it centered about the church. When a German-speaking or Swedish-speaking congregation was organized, its theological creed created little interest. The important thing was that a place existed where the mother tongue was spoken, where one's compatriots gathered from miles around, where customs were familiar. This harmony was oftentimes disturbed by the arrival of missionaries of other sects, who attempted to round up sheep which had strayed; but, in general, the first group upon the scene retained its preëminent position. Around it grew up lay activities which had little or no religious significance: musical clubs, insurance funds, even coöperative merchandising groups.

A favorite occupation of the immigrant intellectual was journalism. The capital outlay was small, for the publisher of an English newspaper was usually willing to allow the Dane or Bohemian to use the shop to print a sheet that would not compete with his own. The non-English communities could support a multitude of weekly and monthly periodicals because many of the foreign newcomers were from the "reading classes." Though they doubtless would have preferred to subscribe for the leading newspaper of the old country, the rates were high and the annual postage of thirty or more dollars a year put the possibility beyond reach. The local editor stepped into the breach, armed with paste pot and shears. Page after page of news, lifted from European sources, attests the continuing interest in the homeland. Once a week, though perhaps two months late, the settler was transported back to the politics and official gossip of the world he had left. This, however, did not last forever. The process of gradual Americanization can be traced, almost measured, by the lengthening columns of American news and, in particular, by the increasing space devoted to the activities and interests of the immigrant group in the United States. Yet the distant continent was never wholly forgotten; and in the years before 1914 probably the class of ordinary American citizens best read in international affairs were not the residents of Boston 'or New York, but the older generation of immigrant farmers in the Middle West.

The newspaper was both an aspect of culture and an instrument of culture. Every alien group bred its own favorite authors. The beginnings were modest. Desiring to set down the experiences of migration, the writers sent their compositions to the editor, who printed them, although they were often little more than incoherent collections of words. Thus started, the literature evolved from poems to stories, from stories to novels, from novels to histories. The student of the future who is willing to conceive of American literature in more than a parochial sense must be the master of at least ten or a dozen languages.

In the fine arts the immigrant made a stronger impact on the native culture. One need not consider the European painter, musician or actor who resided only temporarily in the United States or who, if he remained, continued a part of that international society which revolves around the cultural capitals of the world. Far different was the case of the struggling genius who, swept along by the wave of migration, discovered a field for his talents in the needs of his fellow countrymen. His only reward, however, was apt to be the joy of doing what he wanted in the odd times left over from the practical duties of the farm or the shop. We catch glimpses of him on the pages of village history: the musician who formed an orchestra of two instruments to play at weddings and other community gatherings; the artist who wandered from settlement to settlement, painting altar pieces for the rude boxlike churches; the lover of the drama who transformed a settler's barn into a theater and presented Lessing, Shakespeare, Holberg or Ibsen for the admiration of neighbors.

Among the Germans such activities found strong encouragement from the Turners, members of a gymnastic society which had formed part of the movement for "Young Germany" in the days before 1848. When several members appeared in a settlement in America, they naturally drifted together to enjoy the exercises which had pleased them in other days. Since marching and "turning" were pleasanter when accompanied by song, singing societies sprang up wherever the flag of the Turners was unfurled. A band enlivened things even more. Though an orchestra demanded greater skill and more competent direction, cities such as Cincinnati, St. Louis and Milwaukee presently boasted amateur groups which could render a Beethoven symphony in acceptable style. The Turners in their eagerness to supplement physical culture with intellectual culture always maintained a library, a reading circle and a dramatic club. Though the great era of the Turners fell in the two decades following the Civil War, before that event they had already done much by means of athletic contests and musical competitions to unite the scattered settlements and strengthen the Germanism of each.

In no place did the Germans flourish more than in Cincinnati. Three daily papers in their native tongue offered the news, and a German theater presented nightly the dramatic masterpieces of the fatherland. On Sunday the immigrant could worship in any one of a dozen churches, and his children were taught in a parochial school in the language of their forebears. During the winter there was a constant succession of recitals and lectures by visiting celebrities; and on a summer's evening he could sit in a restaurant garden, sipping beer to the strains of familiar music, and drifting away in thought until the landscape before him was merged into the past, the hills of the Ohio became the hills of the Rhine, and four thousand miles of mountains and ocean ceased to exist.

To some extent, nearly every immigrant nationality managed to perpetuate the atmosphere of the motherland. In this sense, the United States in 1860 was made up not merely of two nations — the North and the South — as is sometimes said, but of many. The North comprised a dozen different peoples who without qualifying their adopted political allegiance lived in the cultural environment of some European nation. What might have been the outcome if the course of development had been uninterrupted no one knows, for the Civil War altered the face of events for both the alien and the native. No ideal of politics, trade or culture was the same after the struggle.

War was the last thing the immigrant had expected in his new home, but the country's ill fortune at least improved his own economic status. Since the Panic of 1857 times had been hard; grain had piled high in every farm building because there was no market. But with the outbreak of hostilities every wagonload of wheat delivered at the railroad commanded a hundred dollars, and every acre of prairie land under the plow yielded a profitable return. The poor immigrant of 1857 was the rich farmer of 1865; and his ardent interest in the culture of the country he had left was cooled by the knowledge that the culture of his adopted country lay now within reach. The family moved into a frame house, leaving the log cabin to stand deserted as a reminder of pioneer beginnings.

Other factors also speeded the war-time Americanization. The older immigrant continued to farm, but his son entered the army. When the village company of volunteers marched away, those who stayed behind went through the routine of seedtime and harvest, but their daily thoughts centered upon the ebb and flow of the campaigns. The past in Europe was overshadowed by the future in America. Four years of anxiety, binding the immigrant family by personal ties to the fortunes of the struggling nation, created a new attitude toward the society which their sons were fighting to preserve.

Only once during the conflict was the loyalty of the foreign citizens called into question. The draft law, adopted in 1863 when the spirit of volunteering had slackened, was not popular in immigrant quarters. The governor of Wisconsin experienced difficulty with the Germans in and about Milwaukee, and for three days the police battled with a mob largely Irish in the streets of New York.[2] But these incidents were exceptional. They merely emphasized the fact that naturalized Americans were making a sacrifice no less costly than that of the native-born. Almost five hundred thousand foreign-born volunteers helped to fight the battles of the Union.[3] No longer could the newcomers be taunted about enjoying the benefits of a government which they had had no hand in creating, for now they were helping to save it.

The Civil War begot a body of tradition in each foreign stock. Though the immigration of nearly every nationality was larger after 1865 than it had been before 1860, no force of numbers could break down the prestige of the war heroes, or change the pattern of thought which the heat of the conflict had stamped on the community. The earlier immigrants had desired to perpetuate a social minority in the American environment; the newer comers, whatever their individual inclinations, were obliged to accept the idea that ultimately their distinctive features would disappear. All they could hope for was to add a bit of their own culture to the amalgam formed by the mingling of many peoples.

[2] F. A. Shannon, *The Organization and Administration of the Union Army* (Cleveland, 1928), II, 205–213, 235–236.
[3] B. A. Gould, *Investigations in the Military and Anthropological Statistics of American Soldiers* (N. Y., 1869), 27.

IMMIGRATION AND AMERICAN CULTURE 143

The Irish were in a strategic position when the war closed, for they had been active both on the field of battle and in the field of politics. Had they directed their energy and influence toward effecting a program of Irishism, their future development might have been different. But they engaged in a crusade of a different sort. Around the camp fires of the Civil War they had repeatedly discussed their native country and its woes. Holding English rule responsible for all of Erin's ills, they resolved on the return of peace to carry on a war for Irish liberation. When the Union forces disbanded in 1865, every soldier carried with him the rifle with which he had fought. Those rifles did good service in the subsequent taming of the West — they fed and protected the homesteaders and guarded the caravans that crossed the plains — but the Irishmen put them to a use of their own. The Fenians, as the Irish Brotherhood called themselves, made two attacks upon Canada and even sent an expedition across the Atlantic.[4] After these fantastic projects failed, Irish energy in America was enlisted in the service of the Land League and, when that had run its course, the war generation was gone. It seems a reasonable conclusion that the preoccupation with agitation for change in Ireland helped to divert attention from the possibility of establishing a more distinct Irish culture in America.

For different reasons the expatriates from the Continent exerted less influence than might be supposed in

[4] L. B. Shippee, *Canadian-American Relations, 1849–1874* (New Haven, 1939), chap. x.

perpetuating their national cultures. This was due in part to the fact that the influx from Germany and Scandinavia consisted largely of young, unmarried men from the rural sections. The new currents in literary and artistic circles had not yet seeped down to the agricultural classes; and the culture these immigrants brought with them was the same as that which had earlier been introduced and modified. Added to this circumstance was the opposition offered by the immigrant churches. Already strongly puritanized, they resisted ideas that were nonreligious in origin and antireligious in aim.

The experiences of the Norwegian, Bjørnstjerne Bjørnson, attest the power of this opposition. In the autumn of 1880 he visited America on a tour of lecturing and observation. He had attacked the church in Norway with bitterness and effect; and in an interview in New York he declared boldly, "I am a freethinker." This phrase every Norwegian pastor used as a text in warning the people against him. As he proceeded on his way west, Bjørnson became increasingly aware of the ecclesiastical ban.[5] When he reached the settlements in Iowa and Minnesota where the Norwegian tongue was as much in use as the English, his audiences and financial receipts dwindled to a point that caused him to abandon the tour. Bjørnson hastened back to Norway eager, as he wrote, to soak himself in a long bath of European culture after the arid months in the American desert.

[5] H. H. Boyesen, "Björnson in the United States," *Critic*, I (1881), 58.

The most obvious sign of the permanence of a non-English-speaking immigrant society appeared in the language. Those who resisted change believed that when language was lost all was lost. On every hand, however, the use of Continental tongues steadily gave way to English and with greatest rapidity in the ordinary associations of daily life. The mother tongue was inadequate to deal with relationships and tasks unknown in the country of origin. Thus there were no words to substitute for settlement, land seeker, pioneer or homestead. Thus, also, the units of measurement were different: miles, bushels, cords, gallons, acres, dollars, cents. In like fashion the farmer worked with new implements: the reaper, the binder, the mower; and he transacted his business at the elevator or the saloon. Foods were also different: beefsteak, bacon, ice cream, oranges, grapes; and drinks as well: cider, lemonade and whisky. It was no use to attempt to translate, for no words were available. The people were obliged to use the vocabulary of the life they lived.

The great shifting of population which took place in the 1870's further weakened the hold of Old World languages. As a result of the free-homestead policy, all the old immigrant communities lost many members of the second generation — the children of the first settlers. Their manner of speech stemmed from family and community habit and, when they moved on, they stepped boldly into the alluring American world. Sometimes, however, the liberation was only temporary because, if they settled in a group, a missionary appeared ere long to plead with them to reaffirm the faith of their fathers by building a church. Once the church was built and a pastor appointed, the new settlement began to receive a share of the continuing stream of immigrants who understood no word of English.

Much of the history of language revolves about the church, and the transformation can be followed most clearly in congregational and synodical records. A distinction must be made between Catholic and Protestant, for though in the end the result was the same, the process was different. The Catholic Church was international, and its traditional policy was to employ the speech of the particular country and to draw its personnel from the people. In the United States, however, administrators and priests had to be obtained where and when they could be found, with the result that the historic practice could not always be followed. Moreover, the language appropriate to the congregations was not always used. At the time that the Catholics consisted principally of Irish and German immigrants, Frenchmen were numerous among the clergy. When Bohemians, Poles and French Canadians constituted the bulk of the Catholic immigrants, Germans and Irish were bishops and priests. A little later, when Italians were being formed into congregations, there were few Italians in the pulpit. Toward the close of the 1880's, the divergence between the shepherds and their flocks was most striking. Factions within the Church demanded that each immigrant community be cared for by priests of its own nationality. Had

"Cahenslyism" won the day, the Catholic Church in the United States would have become a mosaic of national churches, each fostering its own language and customs. But the papacy declined to reverse its historic policy, insisting that ultimately all Catholics in America should be one people just as the Church was one.

In Protestant denominations, where local autonomy permitted the organization to proceed along national lines, foreign speech was more firmly intrenched and change was slower. A city with a large immigrant population might possess separate Lutheran churches for the Germans, Swedes, Danes and Norwegians. Though they had in common the Augsburg Confession, each clung jealously to its own language and special ways — to such an extent, indeed, that eventually the youth rebelled. A home awaited them in the English-speaking Lutheran Church which had existed from the early nineteenth century; and when the drift started, the non-English groups were obliged to make concessions both as to language and as to strictness of doctrine. The process was hastened by the World War and today the transformation is almost complete.

The predominance of English speech was further assured by the large influx from England in the 1870's and 1880's into the upper Mississippi Valley. It is surprising that the English, who have contributed the most to American culture, have been studied the least by students of immigration. There is no English-American historical society, no separate history of the English stock. Discussions of English influence in America are invariably confined to the colonial period and to the legal, economic and social institutions then planted. Such studies ignore the steady inflow of Englishmen that continued all through the nineteenth century with marked effects in anglicizing a region which by 1860 had taken on a Teutonic hue. In the pre-Civil-War period Yankees from the East were amazed to note the change that had come over their Western brethren: their vocabulary and ways of life were all colored by the example of the Germans. Astute Western politicians did not forget the importance of the German vote. Abraham Lincoln tried to master the complexities of German grammar; and prior to his first nomination for the presidency he owned a German-language newspaper for a few months. The swelling flood of immigrants after 1865 seemed likely to intensify the Teutonic character of the region.

Among the factors working against this outcome none was more important than the great increase of English settlers. By 1890 they were to be found in every part of the upper Mississippi Valley. By origin the Englishman was a countryman, born and bred to agricultural life; by intent he became a prairie farmer. Possessing greater initial resources than the Continental immigrant, he made a quicker start at independent farming; and this fact, together with his prior knowledge of the language, placed him on a higher level in community affairs. He did not assert himself belligerently; nor did he suffer from an inferiority complex. His presence created no problem, social or political. If he were a young man (and the large proportion were), no extraneous difficulties hindered his courting the daughter of the American landowner. He quickly melted into the life of the neighborhood.

It is a commonplace of American social history that in the last quarter of the century an "English vogue" characterized all ranks of the people. This circumstance has been variously ascribed to the happy diplomatic relations then prevailing, to the growth of a native aristocracy which looked abroad for its standards, to the personal popularity of the Queen, to the increasing tourist pilgrimages to the shrines of English history and literature. But probably more pervasive than any of these factors was the presence of a million English immigrants. Evidences of this vogue were most conspicuous in the cities, where the daily press made a feature of society news; but the admiration for things English was not restricted to such bounds. The Norwegian novelist, Knut Hamsun, believed he was a competent judge of artistic and cultural matters, yet in the Wisconsin village where he sojourned his opinion counted for naught if an Englishman were present. If you want to compliment an American, he wrote, tell him that you mistook him for an Englishman.[6] So far did the prestige of the country of origin go that, among old and young alike, the tone of society was established by the usages that the English newcomer sanctioned.

[6] Knut Hamsun, *Fra det moderne Amerikas aandsliv* (Copenhagen, 1889), 18.

In the vast economic changes that followed the Civil War the immigrants found an open door to American opportunity in the city as well as in the country. This rapid exploitation of unexampled physical resources was an Americanizing influence of incalculable import. Some of the great entrepreneurs, such as Andrew Carnegie from Scotland, Michael Cudahy from Ireland and John A. Roebling from Germany, were themselves of foreign birth. The bulk of the immigrants, however, played an anonymous part by performing the heavy manual toil. With patient frugality they nursed their small savings in order to assure a better life for their children, if not for themselves.

By the last decade the immigrant generation was beginning to die off, and many of the kings of pork and steel left sons upon thrones that tottered in the depression of 1893. When the new century brought another era of prosperity, the second generation seemed to have forgotten some of the most valuable belongings their fathers had brought with them. But the broader view of history reveals many resurgences of culture after its more obvious signs disappeared. These inheritances from the Old World continue to add richness and variety to the sum total of American life.

The "new" immigration began too late to exert much effect on American life in the nineteenth century. Not until 1882 did the arrivals from Southern and Eastern Europe appear in noticeable numbers, and not until 1896 did they exceed in volume those from Northern and

Western Europe. Their presence intensified many social problems, especially in the cities, and for this reason has tended to obscure the subtler influences they have exercised on American civilization. A single group, that of the Italians, will serve for illustration.

Any appraisal of the contributions made by the many persons of Italian birth must recognize two circumstances that surrounded their coming. They were the first immigrants to arrive in large numbers after the close of the great period of land settlement. Many new and peculiar experiences awaited them, presenting difficulties their predecessors had not been obliged to face. The German or Swede had settled with his wife and children on a Midwestern farm, where the family remained intact in the comparative isolation of a prairie homestead and all the social habits of the family were at first maintained. Change came slowly and the inevitable adjustments were made without much strain. But the Italian family, instead of a hundred and sixty acres, often occupied two or three rooms. Instead of being surrounded by fields it was usually hedged in by slums. This revolution in living conditions brought about a loosening of all the ties that bound the members together. Time-honored ideals were blunted and the traditional culture was quickly forgotten. Only unusual vitality could preserve any part of it.

The other circumstance was the product of recent European conditions. Long before the United States became their destination the Italians had been accustomed to migrate. For twenty years organized bands of laborers had made seasonal visits to Germany and France, and some, more adventurous, had spent several months a year in Latin America. The typical Italian emigrant of the 1890's looked upon his stay abroad as temporary. He delegated to a leader the regulation of most of the arrangements concerning employment, and he was slow in striking roots in the new soil. He did not intend that his residence in the United States should be different from his previous sojournings in France or the Argentine.

In time, however, the force of these two circumstances was overcome. The temporary stay became permanent, and the families tended to drift away from the cities. They transformed vacant lots in the suburbs into market gardens and brought fresh vegetables every day to the housewife's door. By the miracle of hard work they turned sandy wastes into vineyards and berry patches. By patient experimentation they introduced into commercial orchards fruits that the native gardener had long attempted vainly to grow. Others became cooks and confectioners and banished kitchen drudgery by transforming it into an art. American diet is healthier and more varied because of Italian gardeners and Italian cooks.

There were also among them those who had not forgotten what could be done with the needle. Their lace work and draperies were sold, first in the street markets and then in the most exclusive shops. Dexterous fingers and an eye quick to note the least irregularity in pattern led them into the silk mills; and wherever quarries of marble were opened, Italian stone workers cut the blocks.

Moreover, all of them — gardeners, mill hands and quarrymen — flocked to the concert halls and opera houses and provided the largest single contingent to the army of appreciative listeners.

The children and especially the grandchildren of these immigrants are revealing a lively interest in the history, literature and art of the land of their forefathers. Pride in these achievements has not weakened their American patriotism; but they are resolved that in the national culture of the future the warmth and refinement of Mediterranean civilization shall have its place alongside the solid and historic institutions contributed by the colonists and immigrants from Western Europe.

VII

THE SECOND COLONIZATION OF NEW ENGLAND

THE planting of New England is an oft-told tale.[1] Too frequently, however, the theme is exhausted with an account of the first settlers. Yet even this part of the story has bred popular misconceptions. The people who came before 1640 were not the only progenitors of the traditional "Puritans." Cromwell found the Scotch prisoners whom he had taken in the border battles a burden; so he sent them across the Atlantic to his stern friends in New England. Huguenots fled from France and established vineyards along the shores of Narragansett Bay. Persistent Dutchmen moved eastward from the Hudson and built their barns in the valleys of the Berkshires. Ulster Irishmen formed half a dozen communities, taking up those rougher and more barren lands that had been left as islands of wilderness as the first wave of settlement flowed rapidly forward. Frenchmen from Canada fished their way down the coast and others settled on the shores of Lake Champlain. German masons and stone workers were brought in to build up and beautify the prosperous

[1] Professor Hansen himself has dealt with the original colonization of New England in a chapter in Hans Kurath and others, *Handbook of the Linguistic Geography of New England* (Providence, 1939), 62–121. — A. M. S.

town of Boston, and several hundreds were planted as farmers in the woods of Waldoboro in Maine. Rhode Island and Connecticut merchants traded in the ports of southern Ireland and, returning, introduced the Hibernian to his future refuge. But with the possible exception of the last, this colonization had come to an end by the middle of the eighteenth century, and for two generations the New England stock was segregated from the peoples of both the Old and the New World.

It is in these years from about 1760 to 1825 that the New England character, which so profoundly influenced the course of American history in the succeeding decades, was formed. The first colonization was followed by the first Americanization. One may hesitate to express numerically the strength of the various stocks that contributed to the formation of this character and yet recognize that each was strong enough to leave some trait, or shape some feature of growth. One by one, the individual nationalities were lost in the slowly forming mass. The Scots disappeared first. They were men without families, willing workers, and genealogy shows that they were prized as husbands. The Huguenots realized that they were accepted only as Protestants and quickly shed their Gallic traits. The Dutch found it difficult to maintain their ground when the New Englanders, armed with land warrants and clubs, swarmed down on them, and those who were not forced to retreat thought it wise to make family alliances with the invaders. The Germans anglicized their names, and even Waldoboro left no sign of their presence other than wide fields of cabbages and a reputation for delicious sauerkraut that lasted into the second half of the following century. The Catholic Irish, whether few or many, by giving up their religion lost their most distinctive characteristic. The Scotch Irish were the last to go. Their settlements were comparatively small and scattered, but they kept up a constant communication with one another, exchanging ministers and sons and daughters, thereby retaining a solidarity which was only slowly broken. It was a homogeneous New England which in the first half of the nineteenth century blossomed out in that culture of which America is most proud, and it was a homogeneous population that was obliged to face the pioneers of the second colonization.

Pioneers of colonization do not advance with banners and trumpets. Here and there it would be rumored through New England villages that a stranger had arrived in town. It was said he was an Irishman, that he had hired himself out for the season on the farm of Seth Blank. Later it was told that three or four had arrived, that there was no doubt — they *were* Irishmen and they were digging a mill race down at the Center. Then there would appear a ruddy-faced girl, who would take service with the Squire's wife. One of the Irishmen had sent for his sister, and all the Irishmen said they had sisters and cousins who would gladly come over if they could be assured of work.

But how did they come? There were no immigrant ships sailing regularly into the harbor of Boston. Even

THE SECOND COLONIZATION 157

as late as 1841 the British consul in the city reported that no vessels were engaged in the passenger trade between the British Isles and Boston.[2] It was whispered, however, that the business was carried on secretly; that mysterious craft were seen hovering at night off some of the smaller ports; and that in the morning strangers made their way into the interior and toward the metropolis. Evasion of the poor laws, which held shipmasters responsible for the support of passengers who might become destitute, was the motive for these surreptitious dealings.

But relatively few of the invaders began their American career with such adventures. Historically, the immigrant may have been the bearer of civilization to America, but, actually, he was classed with barrels of pork and bales of cotton. Brusque, hard-headed skippers did not realize that upon them had devolved one of the most necessary functions in the spread of European culture. They were going to America for a cargo and, if any emigrants were willing to go where they were going, so much the better. Westward-bound ships usually had to sail in ballast, and passengers were a convenient sort of freight. They loaded and unloaded themselves, fed themselves, shifted themselves in a storm, and could be put to the pumps in an emergency. The ocean paths of German migration may be interpreted in terms of cotton and tobacco, the Irish in terms of lumber. It is probably not an exaggeration to say that Celtic New England is largely the product of the New Brunswick timber trade.

[2] *Parliamentary Papers* (1842), XXXI, 314.

Ireland is the Emerald Isle, but its green is the green of meadows and hedges, not of forests. Tradition tells of the remote time when Ireland was favored with tangled woods and sacred groves; but the Saxon conqueror had destroyed these lurking places, a destruction lamented most by those natives who had an eye for the beautiful. Wood was not an everyday necessity in the huts of laborers and cottiers as long as the peat bogs provided them with fuel. Cottages, however, could not be constructed entirely of mud and stones. There had to be some beams, and the difficulty in securing timbers was often the only obstacle that prevented the establishing of a household. When tenants were ejected and their huts razed, even the most flinty-hearted landlord allowed them to bear off these precious beams without which they could have no roof over their heads when they squatted on the waste by the roadside or on the edge of the bog. A growing population and an increasing number of households demanded a continual importation of timber. Moreover, the packing of butter, salt pork and eggs for sale in England demanded firkins, hogsheads and crates. The cooperage industry was flourishing, and by 1830 every seaport village in the south and west had its merchants who in the spring of the year sent out their vessels to the St. Lawrence, where the forests grew down to the water's edge.

For the emigrant the advantages offered by these vessels were many. No long journey to the unknown ports of Dublin or Londonderry was necessary in order to board them. Moreover, the route was cheap: instead of the four or five pounds charged for passage to New York, the rate to the maritime provinces sometimes was as low as fifteen shillings. The time was shorter, so the bag of potatoes need not be so full, nor the salted herring so many. Every vessel was in a hurry to load its cargo of deals and lumber and, as soon as he trod American soil, the passenger was sure of employment that continued throughout the summer. But when the last vessel had returned and the immigrant faced the winter, the prospects were not so encouraging. He could go to the woods as a lumberman, and often did, but the experience seldom left any desire for a second season. He might go into the bush and take up land, but before any acres had been cleared the social instincts of the Irishman usually revolted. Sooner or later he turned his mind toward the "States," whence came stories of employment, high wages and friends who had discovered prosperity. Therefore he set out for the south.

The simplest way was to walk. Thousands did — following the coast of New Brunswick to Maine and continuing along the trails and roads into the populous parts of New England. Many of these travelers found work with farmers along the way and attached themselves to the communities through which they passed. The pioneer Catholic churches in Maine clearly define this route. But the majority had a more distant object in view and had no communication with the natives except to ask for food or shelter. The possibilities of such assistance were well recognized, and the master of the ship *Ocean*, when he advertised its forthcoming departure, pointed out the advantages of this route, "those living on that line of road being very kind to Strangers as they pass."[3]

Such a tedious journey, however, might be avoided. At the international boundary separating Maine and New Brunswick the British timber trade met the American coasting trade. This trade was very lively. Agriculture in the Eastern states had risen above frontier methods, and science and necessity were impressing upon the farmer the need of fertilizing his soil. But the only mineral fertilizer with which agriculture was acquainted was gypsum, or plaster of Paris, of which large supplies were available in Nova Scotia. From the mines it was brought to Eastport and Passamaquoddy and there transferred to the American coasting vessels which gathered in great numbers. These ships were not equipped to carry passengers, but the immigrants asked for no equipment but a deck. For a small sum they were transported to Newburyport, Boston, Providence and New London, whence they scattered in search of employment. Had the Canadian timber trade and its extensions not existed, New England would undoubtedly have been flooded with immigrants; but the supply of labor would have been drawn from the port of New York and its composition would have been more varied, such as that which advanced from New York into the Middle West. It was the timber trade that made New England overwhelmingly Irish.

The tasks that employed these foreigners are part of

[3] *Galway Free Press*, March 28, 1835.

the economic history of the section. They dug canals, built railroads, excavated for foundations, constructed wharves, and acted as laborers, stevedores and porters. Not many of them were mechanics and few Americans felt their competition, for they performed services that the natives were unable or unwilling to render. Their employment in gangs upon the public works and their concentration in the poorer quarters of the cities or in the shanty towns upon the outskirts drew public attention, then and since, from the many who scattered through the interior. The farmer of southern New England was losing his traditional "help," for the young man of New Hampshire or Vermont who had formerly hired out for a season or two before setting up for himself, now was going West or becoming a clerk or mechanic in the city. So the farmer was forced to take the Irishman, although he complained about his awkwardness in handling the plow and the oxen, accused him of laziness when he waited for specific directions regarding what was to be done, and hesitated to accept as a member of the family one so alien in customs and attitudes. By 1853 foreign farm laborers predominated in the eastern counties of Massachusetts and they were appearing in the hill towns of the interior.

Tradition has little pleasant to say regarding these Irish immigrants. They were regarded as stupid and dirty, superstitious and untrustworthy, diseased and in despair. They were viewed as beggars and thieves, the overflow of Irish poorhouses and outcasts from overpopulated estates.

Without question, persons illustrating these characteristics were among them, but the tradition descends from one season and slanders those who came before and those who followed. The spring of 1847 witnessed a flight from famine and fever which brought thousands to die in the slums and gutters of American cities and other thousands to beg their way from town to town and to spread pestilence. But before that year the immigrant was either the more ambitious son, who saw no prospects for himself in his native land, or the "small declining farmer," who saw no prospects for his family. In the years that followed that fatal season, especially from about 1850, he was the tenant who before the famine had enjoyed a certain comfort, but who now, with depleted resources, was unable to maintain his position in the new order of Irish life. For now the potato was destroyed, the corn laws that had protected him in the British market were repealed, and his holding was burdened with a new poor law which saddled upon him the obligation of supporting those of his neighbors who had managed to survive the years 1847 and 1848 with property and health gone.

The Irish of the great exodus did not expect to live at ease upon the bounty of a charitable people, or to be content in the cellars and shacks of a Little Dublin. They were seeking, first, a material existence independent of the whims of both landlords and Nature and, second, a respected position in a democratic society. These ends were achieved in a surprisingly short time. The natural course of events coöperated with individual endeavor to elevate the group as a whole. Before native philanthropy was aroused or the newcomers had organized for mutual assistance, changes in climate, overwork, homesickness and discouragement had carried through the cruel process of killing off those who should never have undertaken the adventure. When the sick, the beggars and the derelicts had been eliminated, the remainder received a popular, though grudging, recognition of the station which their patience and industry had won.

They had done no more than to make the most of the opportunities that were offered. In their progress upward through the mills they started literally in the basement. When there were no more foundations to be laid, there were more machines to be operated, and the supply of young ladies of Yankee blood proved unequal to the demand. Irishmen were taken into the new factories; and in many cities and villages there existed, side by side, older establishments, in which the operatives were the traditional visitors from the New England farms, and newer, in which foreigners predominated. But the former class had never been permanent; after earning a dowry, they went back to a country home of their own. But now their younger sisters refused to take the vacant places in the mills. To some extent, this disinclination resulted from an aversion to being classed economically with the aliens whom popular opinion had taught them to despise; but the aversion was strengthened by the possibility of securing employment as teachers and clerks and in the many varied opportunities which a more complex economic system provided. So in time the Irishman manned the older mills as well, and by 1860 the second stage in the history of the New England mill population had been reached. The operatives were Irish.

This conquest naturally gave them a stability which affected all features of their life. In Ireland the tenant had learned to save. A few shillings from eggs and butter, a pound from the pig, a guinea or two earned by harvest labor went to pay the rent. The cash income of the Irish cottage was small, but a remarkably large proportion of it was handed over to the manager of the estate. In crossing the Atlantic this habit persisted. There was, of course, a class which was dazzled by the wealth that flowed into their pockets from the public works and spent it recklessly; but this class eliminated itself by riotous living. The majority put the dollars away under the eaves until they were sufficient to buy a passage for parents or brothers at home. After the first comers had transported an army of relatives across the Atlantic, the savings banks began to prosper; and in time the individual accumulations reached an amount that tempted the possessors to think of houses and lands.

Unfortunately, most of the town sites belonged to factory owners, who hesitated to sell them while the capital invested in boarding houses and tenements yielded so high and steady a return. The home seeker was forced to go out to the edge of the city, where the family combined the functions of mill operatives and market gardeners. But this step had distinct disadvantages, and many, who otherwise would have put their savings into a cottage and continued in the factory, used these savings to establish themselves in mercantile and semiprofessional pursuits. A more liberal policy on the part of the corporations would have prevented the rapid increase of corner saloons and preserved many modest fortunes that were wrecked in the unfamiliar world of business.

The transformation of this immigrant group into farmers did not proceed so rapidly. That the Irishman, who at home had fought and bled for the privilege of renting a quarter of an acre of land, should in America refrain from seizing the almost free lands of the West, has always been accounted a mystery. But the mystery is not so dark that it cannot at least be partially understood. The abstinence was not as complete as has been supposed. Irishmen did become farmers — as every county history of the Middle West proves. The typical immigrant who dug canals in Ohio or built railroads in Illinois followed a course of evolution which turned him into a farmer on the cheap lands near the scene of his labor. This step was as logical for him as the movement into the mills was for his brother in New England, for the Irishman in the East was too canny to pass over a steady wage in the factory in order to undertake farming in a region where everyone was talking of the decadence of agriculture. He could have gone West, but the Irishman not only loved land, he also loved company, and all that he heard about the prairies — distances without end, villages without society, no churches of his faith — persuaded him to remain where he was. Under the impact of the industrial depression of the late fifties a movement to rural New England began. Americans of older stock complained that the farms were passing into the hands of an alien people and the Yankee yeomanry was becoming a thing of the past. The transformation was impending, but at the opening of the Civil War the recolonization of rural New England had hardly commenced.

Irishmen were not the only strangers to find their way to New England before the Civil War. But the normal course of commerce did not bring Germans and Scandinavians to her ports, and contractors who experimented with importing them as laborers discovered that Corkonians and Far-Downers, who usually found it difficult to live in peace with each other, willingly joined forces to break the heads of those impudent foreigners who dared to take the bread out of their mouths. In the more technical phases of industry, however, Germans found a place, and by 1850 there were nearly two thousand of them in Boston and its vicinity and others scattered throughout the factory towns of the Connecticut Valley.[4] But the mass migration of this element to America did not get under way until the early fifties, and by that time the laboring opportunities of New England had been preëmpted, its agricultural character blackened and a reputation for inhospitality achieved. In 1852, when a shipload of Germans disembarked at Boston, they piled their heavy chests upon wagons and, forming a proces-

[4] *Massachusetts Public Documents for 1855*, 99.

sion, marched across the city to the railroad cars that would transport them to the West, flaunting a sign which bore the inscription: "Hail, Columbia, Land of the Free. We will be no burden to Massachusetts."

The Civil War marked the close of the distinctly Irish phase of the second colonization. Irish continued to come, but in that steady and unvarying current which represents a migration in which each individual has had the way prepared for him by a predecessor. The war checked what had promised to be a general movement to the land. It brought an unheard-of prosperity to a people who were safely beyond poverty; and it induced a more varied industrial activity and, because of the scarcity of hands, forced an increasing use of the foreign-born in manufactures. When peace returned, the immigrants were more than ever colonists, for instead of being participants in a few simple economic activities they were now firmly rooted in all. They were also more a part of that spiritual entity which makes up a nation. During the war a few score of them had been politicians, and tens of thousands of them soldiers. In the heat of the conflict Know-Nothingism had been forgotten, not only at the front, but also among those at home who shared a common anxiety and often the sorrows of a common sacrifice.

It was soon apparent that the war-time labor shortage was to be permanent. Both farm and factory were affected. The youth who returned from the army did not go back to his home in the hills. Many went to the West; perhaps more settled in the cities. Help for the harvest season could be secured only at rates that were ruinous when income and expenditures were compared at the close of the year. At the gatherings of agricultural societies the problem of hired hands loomed as the most pressing. In the cities the older operatives were passing beyond the productive age, and the sons of these immigrants, as well as the recruits from the country, found it possible to start on a higher rung of the economic ladder. When the farmers said that their only hope lay in immigration, they expressed a sentiment that the manufacturers repeated more loudly and more effectively.

In the great flood of migration which in the years after the war swept from Europe to America there was one current which flowed silently and swiftly, and quickly lost itself as it spread out over the continent. This was the English. Beside it there were a German stream, a Swedish and a Norwegian, and a dozen minor currents that can be traced not only to New York, but to the pools which they formed in the Mississippi Valley. But in the twenty years from 1870 to 1890 more Englishmen crossed the Atlantic than Scandinavians or, probably, Germans. Of this influx New England might have had a share, for the English factory worker as well as the agricultural laborer took part in the movement. Indeed, when the industrial boom was under way, the Fall River industrialists encouraged spinners and weavers from Lancashire to enter their employ. But they soon decided they had made a mistake. Many of the craftsmen came from parts which had engaged in bitter class strife. They brought with them their discontent, an inherited distrust of all capitalists, and the idea that "a strike was as natural as a day's rest on Sunday."[5] For a year or two the city was in turmoil, with the result that the employers henceforth excluded English operatives from their plants.

The Chinese were suggested as a labor force. They were docile, patient workers who did not watch the clock, frugal livers who did not demand exorbitant wages, stolid beings who could not be swayed by the agitator. Their advocates foretold a New England in which factory wheels would turn steadily, the laboring class live simply and contentedly, and their employers divide their time between the management of these patriarchal mills and the higher arts of civilization. It was a curious state of mind for a people who had just rescued one race from slavery. Farmers, also, brightened at the prospect. The wonders of Chinese agriculture were recounted, the more conservative were urged to give up their race prejudices, and some were known to repeat with favor the sentiment credited to the labor captains of California: "All I want in my business is muscle. I don't care whether it be obtained from a Chinaman or a white man — from a mule or a horse!"[6]

The experiment was actually made. At great expense two carloads of Chinese were transported from California to North Adams, Massachusetts, and placed in a shoe fac-

[5] Massachusetts Bureau of Statistics of Labor, *Thirteenth Annual Report* (1882), 340.
[6] Secretary of the Connecticut Board of Agriculture, *Tenth Annual Report* (1876–1877), 48.

tory which had been troubled by strikes and labor discontent. The result was discouraging. The Orientals died, wandered away, or hung on listlessly. Sociologists pointed out the dangers inherent in the situation, while merchants complained that they were favored with no trade. Still there was no enthusiasm for the English, and soon they were completely forgotten when New England realized that at its door it possessed a limitless supply of workers whom a phrase-maker dubbed "the Chinese of the Eastern States." [7]

French Canada had been on the point of swarming before the Civil War, but the first contact of Irish and Canadians had not been peaceful. Now Quebec was bursting with young men, and even the influence of the Catholic Church, which tried to direct the emigrants toward the West, was not strong enough to keep them out of New England. At first, they were looked upon with some disfavor by employers as being unaccustomed to machinery and unreliable; but experience revealed that, if recognition were given to certain holidays, they worked contentedly the rest of the time. They came from the north dressed in jeans and moccasins; within six months they were as a class the best purchasers of the latest goods on the market. Being acceptable to both employers and merchants, they were doubly welcome. Agents were sent to the provinces to stimulate the movement and, as the older Irish group died out, the mills gradually became French.

[7] Massachusetts Bureau of Statistics of Labor, *Twelfth Annual Report* (1881), 469.

Hitherto this second colonization, with the exception of market gardeners and a few adventurers, had left the rural regions in the possession of the native stock. Farm laborers of foreign birth came and went, only occasionally attaching themselves to the community. In the meantime agricultural New England was entering upon its great decline. Upper hillside farms were abandoned and cabins left tenantless; cultivated clearings became brush pastures; scrub oaks, alders and chestnuts grew up in the decaying orchards. Year by year the average of the farm population became older and older, and, lacking energy, indulged in "skinning" — mowing the natural meadows and selling the hay, and cutting off the timber for which a profitable market existed in the neighboring cities. The old men and old women hung on, refusing to leave the ancestral estate until that Providence, which almost three hundred years before had sent a plague to dispose of the savages in order that the Pilgrims and their neighbors might find cornfields already cleared, now visited New England with another scourge. Some blamed the overeating of watermelons; others ascribed it to the pollution of the rivers. Whatever the cause, in the late eighties the New England hills were rocked with malaria and ague which shook loose the venerable descendants of the first occupiers and prepared the way for their successors.

The depression that followed 1893 is as important for the history of American agriculture as of industry. Just like its predecessors, it forced a movement to the land, but this time not to the West. Kansas and Nebraska had little to offer; and the now unemployed factory worker, who had patiently saved with the intention of some day buying land, had to choose between remaining in the city and eating up his bank account, or locating upon one of the much maligned abandoned farms of the East. He chose the latter. This drift is hard to measure, but into the reports of agricultural societies and onto the pages of farm journals there creeps a note of optimism. The repopulation of the New England countryside had begun. City magnates, coming back to their birthplace for the Old Home Week festivities, commented on the degeneration that accompanied this foreign occupation: unpainted houses, devastated woodlands, broken fences. But the agents who had negotiated the transactions and the bankers who held the mortgages knew that the degeneration had preceded the foreign invasion; in fact, it was the only thing that brought the land within the immigrant's financial reach. They pointed to fields of tobacco and onions and rows of vegetables, where whole families crawled on their knees, and declared that the revival of New England agriculture was under way because it had adjusted itself to new conditions and had come into the hands of those who would work as hard as the first lords of the soil had worked and were willing to endure the same privations. The last stronghold of the ancient inhabitants had fallen.

After 1900 the second colonization entered upon its third phase. The first phase had been predominantly Irish, the second predominantly French; now the immigration was of a more varied composition. Portuguese took up the lands on Cape Cod. Finns and Swedes settled in the more northern sections. Greeks and Syrians formed colonies in certain manufacturing centers. Italians appeared in all cities and villages, and from New York came Jewish farmers. But none of these arrived in such numbers as to dominate one area or one activity, and their appearance is so recent that they are still in the first period of their adjustment.

The present federal immigration policy has put an end to the second colonization. The process of amalgamation will proceed with the stocks already in New England. The ratio of births and deaths, however, among the descendants of the first and second colonizations is so different that the influence of the second will continue to become proportionally greater. In time, the class that produced the cultured New England of the last century will be submerged by their successors, considered to be a motley folk with no literature, no art, no philosophy. There are those who see in the transformation a cause for despair; but it must be recalled that almost a hundred years elapsed from the close of the first colonization until the civilization that it produced attained its finest expression. The elements that entered into the second, while perhaps potentially more capable, are more varied, less experienced, and have suffered from the tradition which viewed their pioneers as ditch diggers and human mechanisms whose contribution, like that of a spade or a dredge, was limited to the physical world. Among these pioneers was one who foresaw the years that must pass before their contribution could be any different, but he left an encouragement for the future:

The fine action of genius is very pleasant, but the hard effort of labor must come first. The pioneer and settler must be in advance of the artist and the author; the sounds of music must come after the echoes of the axe; the painter must be in the wake of the hunter; the ploughman must be before the poet; and the hut must be the herald of the temple.[8]

[8] Henry Giles, *Lectures and Essays on Irish and Other Subjects* (N. Y., 1869), 156.

VIII

MIGRATION ACROSS THE NORTHERN BORDER

TO THE census taker every Canadian in the United States and every American in Canada has been a statistic. To the historian he has been a human being who aimed not to illustrate the laws of population, but to make a living or find adventure. The North American of the nineteenth century had a restless spirit and a wandering foot. He cut his way through the forest and beat a track across the plains. He traversed mountains and forded rivers. He passed from the jurisdiction of the United States to that of the British Crown; and often he, his son or his grandson went back to the land of their fathers. The international boundary proved the least troublesome of the barriers created by Nature or by man that fell athwart his path.

Today historians wish they knew more about him and the apparently erratic course he followed. Sooner or later, he ended up in a place called the frontier; but what the frontier exactly was and how the pioneer got there and what he was like upon arrival they do not know. Had enumerators been stationed at the mountain passes and river crossings, it would be possible to trace his journeys, though the pioneer was not easy to count even when he crossed from one country to another. After the Civil War the American authorities undertook to report upon the number of Canadian-born persons entering the country, and the Canadian officials, alarmed by the statistics, did some counting of their own.[1] Evidently some difference of opinion existed as to the identity of the settler. Thus the American figures for 1884, covering the arrivals at Port Huron and Detroit, showed a total of forty-nine thousand, whereas the Canadian estimate placed the number at four thousand.

During the last decade or two, historians have given increasing attention to the technique and significance of population movements. From land deeds, tax lists, church records and muster rolls and from the labors of the too-much-despised genealogist they are gradually piecing together a mosaic which, in time, will reveal the pattern of the original agricultural settlement of the continent. When viewed against the background of this mosaic, it is likely that many familiar episodes of American history will assume new proportions and new relationships and that the rôle of language, nationality and religion as factors influencing group action will be more understandable. However, little was permanent in the life of the New World. The mosaic becomes a kaleidoscope and the historian's eye must be trained to catch the shifting pattern and note the changes in nationality and grouping that modified the original scene. No analysis of a historical

[1] M. L. Hansen, *The Mingling of the Canadian and American Peoples* (New Haven, 1940), chaps. ix–x.

development is complete without a recognition of this population factor; and no population study of historical interest is complete if it ignores the fact that the Canadian-American boundary, which meant so much to the diplomat, legislator and tradesman, was nonexistent in the consciousness of the unnumbered hundreds of thousands who were doing the principal job of the century — turning the wilderness into farms and homes.

Population has expanded from the Atlantic to the Pacific and the main currents of this movement, together with the eddies set up along their fringes, have been a constant force leading to the transformation of the original settlements. The development of industries has, at certain times and in certain places, slowed down the current, or diverted it from its normal course. The greater division of labor that substituted the city for the village as the center of commercial life brought about a rearrangement of people. The westward movement, industrialization and urbanization — these are the three grand divisions into which the population history of both the United States and Canada falls. A brief survey of the evolution of these features will illustrate the continental character of this basic aspect of their common history.

During that era of American history known as the colonial period, the popular advice was not, "Young man, go west." In New England the counsel was, "Go north," and in the valleys of the Hudson and Delaware and beyond it was, "Go south." So far as the West was concerned, Nature, the Indians and imperial policy warned, "Keep out!" The Atlantic was still the great highway, and along the coast and up and down the rivers passed not only ships of commerce, but sloops, dugouts and canoes bearing families of settlers, household goods and cattle. From the waterside they struck out into the hills and followed the ridges and valleys, the lines of migration gradually weaving a close network of rather small farms peopled by a sturdy stock which doubled in numbers in less than a quarter of a century. Although none went west, this was Chapter One of the westward movement, because it was the process which established the firm base that was to support the spectacular march which in less than a hundred years carried the pioneers from the crest of the Alleghenies to the shores of the Pacific.

The interdependence of areas which later became parts of the United States and the Dominion of Canada is illustrated even during this preliminary period. Many of the non-*Mayflower* colonists of New England sailed on fishing boats for the Newfoundland Banks, where they transferred to the smaller craft that had come up from Salem and Boston. Later, when French Acadia had become British Nova Scotia, Halifax was a recognized steppingstone for emigrants from the mother country bound for any of the colonies. The trend, however, turned decidedly in the opposite direction when the expulsion of the Acadians opened up for settlement the fields and meadows they had occupied and the adjacent lands, now free from the menace of hostile neighbors. For several years after 1759, farmers of Pennsylvania, New Jersey and New England sailed off on colonizing ventures to the northeast and planted a dozen vigorous communities of pioneer stock about the Bay of Fundy. Very often they set forth at the same time as friends who were bound for the fertile valleys of Maine and with whom they parted company when near the mouth of the Androscoggin or the Penobscot. Whether the destination was Maine or Nova Scotia, the historical rôle of the individual was the same. He was part of the great northward surge of population that filled in the last unoccupied area of the Atlantic base.

At the close of the war with France in 1763 it was expected that a similar movement would proceed up the Hudson-Richelieu waterway and take possession of that part of the St. Lawrence Valley which the French had not yet reached. Imperial policy favored an expansion of this nature. The provisions of the Proclamation of 1763 encouraging the Yankee to take up the valley lands were sound in geography as well as in statesmanship; but the Yankee did not come. The time was not yet ripe, and political considerations carried some weight. Twenty years later the Loyalists, honored in song and story, performed this logical task at the logical time. If their special hardships and unusual fortitude be forgotten, the Loyalists were just a group of American pioneers engaged in the business of inheriting the earth. When their epic was finished, every strategic point was in possession of the European; and the conquest of the interior of the continent could begin.

The westward movement was not a uniform advance

along a front of a thousand miles. The conquering pioneer, no matter how individual a skirmisher he felt himself to be, belonged to one of four main columns into which Nature divided the army. The first of these columns swung in a great semicircle through the South Atlantic states and along the coast of the Gulf of Mexico. The second cut diagonally through the southern mountains into Tennessee and the old Southwest. The third chose the valley of the Ohio. The fourth took the highway marked by the Great Lakes. From each of these columns brigades, regiments and solitary patrols broke away to follow their own course up an attractive valley or along a belt of fertile soil. It was the peculiar relation of the fourth of the columns to the international boundary which made the westward movement such a significant factor in the joint history of the United States and Canada.

By 1790 New England and many parts of New York had reached a stage of development when an outpouring of people was inevitable. This impulse started the column upon its march. A flank movement, at the very beginning, diverted many of the New Englanders into the region south of the St. Lawrence known as the Eastern Townships of Quebec. The main body continued due west along the Mohawk and filled in the Genesee Country of western New York and the plain south of Lake Ontario. But some in the ranks had relatives and former neighbors among the Loyalists. Time had softened political feeling; blood and early friendship reasserted themselves. These people found homes, society and institutions to their liking in the province of Upper Canada. There were, in fact, some decided advantages in the more peaceful Indian relations and the more generous terms of acquiring land. All this was duly reported "back home" and, when the column reached Niagara and had to decide whether to continue north or south of Lake Erie, the decision was in favor of the former. During the ten years preceding the outbreak of the War of 1812, Upper Canada was rapidly settled, the majority of the arrivals being emigrants from the Republic, who changed their allegiance with apparent unconcern.

When the war ended, Americans received less of a welcome, and the British government adopted a positive plan of peopling its colony with the unemployed and unlanded inhabitants of the British Isles. Moreover, the war had removed the Indian menace in Indiana and Illinois and, accordingly, the column now chose these territories as a destination. For twenty-five years, except for merchants and professional men, the mingling of peoples along the border was negligible. But by the early 1830's hard times had struck the upper province; a generation of typical pioneer agriculture had depleted the soil; large families had cleared every acre of woodland that could be put under the plow. The traditional remedy for the traditional ills of frontier farming was to go west; but the province had no west. Hence after 1837, when economic gloom deepened the pessimism that resulted from what seemed to be an unsuccessful struggle for political rights, the Canadian farmer broke camp and hastened to join his comrade, the American pioneer, who had now reached the prairies of Wisconsin and Iowa. A characteristic flank movement had turned northward into Michigan and here, where timber, soil and climate were similar to what they had always known, the Canadians found a promised land within a few days' journey by wagon or by foot. They made of the Detroit River a Canadian stream and fringed the peninsula with colonies of fishermen, farmers and woodsmen.

The two decades between 1840 and 1860 constitute a period marked by great exploits of courage and adventure. They form the heroic chapter in the history of the American West. But there was no achievement of this colorful era which the Canadian did not share. Gold was discovered in California, and from the seaports and farms of the provinces, as from the seaports and farms of the states, young men rushed by land and water to the diggings. Then gold was discovered in British Columbia, and the men, now a little older, rushed across the boundary into the jurisdiction of the British Crown. In the rugged country south of Lake Superior copper and iron were found and, in response to the call for laborers, Canadian trappers left the woods to handle the pick alongside miners from Pennsylvania and Cornwall. The new homes on the prairies could not be built without the lumber from the northern forests, and in the company of experienced choppers from Maine came the loggers and rivermen of New Brunswick. Fishermen from the lower St. Lawrence set up their reels on the shores of Lake Michigan and Lake Huron; and on the hundreds of vessels that bore the commerce of the Lakes were scores of captains and thousands of sailors who had learned navigation in the waters surrounding Nova Scotia.

For Americans the excitement of these decades was forgotten in the greater excitement of the Civil War. The four years of that struggle constitute an interlude in the normal development of the continent. Like all other relations, those concerning population were affected by the fears and fortunes of the conflict. Young men in the provinces, eager for adventure and attracted by the promise of substantial bounties, left home to join the Union armies, and en route they passed draft dodgers who were "skedaddling" across the border in an effort to elude pursuing marshals. War-time need caused a shortage of laborers, skilled and unskilled, and Canadian artisans and farm hands, when they learned of the high wages paid in the fields and factories of the Northern states, hastened to make the most of the opportunities. But few of those who moved in either direction remained permanently. Soldiers and workmen were discharged and went back to Canada; "skedaddlers" were forgiven and returned home.

Not the circumstances of the war, but the results of the war, marked the beginning of a new phase in the population relations of the two countries. Now at last the trans-Mississippi West was open for occupation. The slavery dispute was settled; the homestead act offered free lands; the Indian menace was removed; a transcontinental railroad was being built. From the defeated South and the victorious North homesteaders poured out onto the plains. The Canadian farmer caught the restless spirit and he, too, set forth to pioneer on this new frontier.

By 1890 almost a million persons of Canadian birth resided in the United States. Of these, more than a third were located in the states and territories of the Middle West. The extent of the exodus alarmed the officials of the new Dominion and, as a countermeasure, they proposed a program for developing their own west, hitherto inaccessible: a transcontinental railroad, the organization of new provinces, a land policy even more liberal than that of the neighboring Republic. The provinces were created and the land law was adopted, but the construction of the railroad lagged. Unless he was willing to face the dangers and difficulties of the primitive trail of lakes and rivers which led from Lake Superior to Winnipeg, there was only one route by which the ambitious Canadian could reach his destination, and that route lay through the United States. The railroads encouraged this transit and the government at Washington placed no obstacles in its way. Special colonist trains were run from Toronto, via Chicago and St. Paul, to the banks of the Red River of the North, where the passengers were transferred to steamers that carried them to Winnipeg. To this convenience was added freedom from the usual annoyance of customs inspection, for the American authorities allowed the settlers' goods to pass through the states in bond. Unfortunately, no records show how many tens of thousands of Canadian migrants enjoyed the hospitality of the neighboring country while passing from east to west, but it is certain that without this hospitality the development of the Red River country and its hinterland would have been retarded a decade or more.

Probably there was policy as well as hospitality involved. Minnesota and the Territory of Dakota also needed men and capital. The resources of Ontario could be as valuable when planted south of "forty-nine" as north of it. At every railroad stop and at the river landing the train was besieged by high-pressure agents of land companies and by citizens who had farms for sale. It was estimated that approximately five per cent of those who entered the United States with the intention of passing on to Manitoba were persuaded that a better fortune awaited them in the Republic. As a result, a considerable aggregation of Canadians was established in the American part of the Red River Valley; and they, together with their compatriots north of the line and the Yankees who were spread up and down the valley, constituted an international community that all but disregarded the boundary. They traveled back and forth, homesteaded on one side of the line, sold their improvements to a later comer, and then moved over to homestead on the other side. Pioneers always saw better opportunities just beyond the horizon, and Canadians and Americans went from one country to the other as light-heartedly as though they were moving from one county to another.

The completion of the Canadian Pacific Railroad in 1885 made the westward advance in both the Dominion and the United States more of a distinctively national movement. In the latter, it slowed down as the more desirable lands were occupied; in the former, the eastern provinces and Europe provided the settlers. For twenty years the historic column seemed to be permanently divided, but it came together again when, at the turn of the century, the rural homes of the Middle West found themselves filled with young people who knew no occupation but farming and whose chief ambition was to acquire a quarter section of virgin soil. The American West had no undeveloped area to match the prairie provinces of Canada and, since the world offered a market for every bushel of wheat that could be grown, the last great agrarian trek began. By train and prairie schooner the Americans moved in and occupied great stretches of Alberta and Saskatchewan. During the fifteen years before the World War nearly a million souls participated. The stock and equipment they carried with them averaged a thousand dollars a family, but no value could be put upon the experience and skill which every able-bodied person contributed.

With this conquest the column all but lost its identity. The majority of the settlers stayed where they first drove in their stakes; and when the sons were ready to leave home, they either moved to the north or responded to the call of industry or commerce. Only a remnant reformed ranks and crossed the mountains to the valleys of British Columbia. Here was much to satisfy them, but agriculture was difficult and in commercial fruit raising they had had no experience. But now there no longer was a West to attract them further on, and those who did not adjust activities to existing opportunities took the only road that remained open. They drifted down the coast to Washington, Oregon and California, where they were lost in the great mingling of people who had gathered on the shores of the Pacific. With their disappearance the westward movement ceased to be a factor in Canadian-American relations.

Its place as a significant force had already been taken by the two other developments that were affecting the course of continental population distribution: industrialization and urbanization. The Canadian whom we have thus far considered was the one of British descent. His French-speaking neighbor was destined for another rôle, a fate the more surprising in view of the rural nature of his background and training. In 1840 there was every indication that the pioneering qualities he had developed in cutting his way back from the St. Lawrence would be put to service in the new lands of the West. Colonies of French Canadians were formed in Illinois, Michigan and Wisconsin, and to observers these settlements seemed the beginning of an emigration from Quebec which would rival any that the neighboring province could send out. But many circumstances of society and economic life made it difficult for the young Frenchman to take permanent leave of the parental roof. The young British Canadian had only one obligation and that was to relieve his parents of the burden of his support. The young

Frenchman, however, felt obliged to contribute to the cash income that was becoming increasingly necessary in the economy of the household. What he desired was a job with wages, good hard cash delivered into his hand on Saturday night. When the opportunity for such payment arose within what to his sturdy legs was walking distance, the attraction of the West dimmed.

French Canadians were not unknown in and about the mills of New England before 1860. During the Civil War they became more numerous, but not until twenty years later did they become predominant, supplanting and sometimes driving out the native Yankee and the immigrant Irishman in many communities.[2] They were more docile than the other workers; and when seasonal or cyclical unemployment appeared, it did not breed the usual social difficulties because so many of them returned to the shelter of the home village back in the seigniories. During the eighties, when the expanding West absorbed the products of the factories, the French Canadian conquered the textile mills and several other branches of factory activity. Like his predecessors, he then set about making himself and his family part of the life to which their fortunes were attached. He contributed to the building of a church and a school, he bought a house and lot, and on Sunday afternoons he strolled through the countryside, pausing to look at the unpainted buildings and the overgrown fields that marked the abandoned

[2] H. F. Wilson, *The Hill Country of Northern New England* (N. Y., 1936), 161–163, 266–267.

farm which New England publicists were deploring. Like many another immigrant, he thought of buying a few acres and leaving the factory for good, and sometimes did so. But the Province of Quebec was close, visits over the border had been frequent, and the officials of the Church and province had become alarmed at the loss that French Canada was suffering. Many retired workers took the savings of ten or a dozen years and, perhaps with ten or a dozen American-born children, returned to the Dominion to pioneer in the forests surrounding Lake St. John, in the upper valley of the Ottawa or, occasionally, on the prairies of the West.

Homesickness for the country into whose allegiance they had been born — a homesickness which the European immigrant felt as strongly but could not allay because of the three thousand miles of water that rolled between the Old World and the New — was the fundamental motivating cause. But it was kept alive and turned into action by the official encouragement known as "repatriation," which both the Province of Quebec and the Dominion of Canada extended. Agents of the respective departments of immigration traveled from mill town to mill town, reawakened the patriotism of youth and, when the day set for the return came, one of them appeared to act as guide. Official coöperation often took the welcome form of part payment of the cost of transportation, special concessions in acquiring land and a supervision which eased the innumerable and unexpected crises of a pioneer's experience. An appreciable proportion of the industrial migrants were migrants two ways, though most of them remained in the new land.

Every Canadian who settled in the United States and every American who went to the Dominion undoubtedly thought of his motives and experiences as unique. But the historian can usually classify him, and these classifications are associated with some of the fundamental transformations of North American society. The crossing and recrossing of the boundary were not part of a haphazard, aimless wandering. They represented a search for the opportunities offered by land, factories and cities. Fortunately, the governments of the two nations did not add to the difficulties by imposing artificial or selfish restrictions; and the people themselves were not hindered by sentiment. The farmer emigrating from east to west, the artisan in search of a factory job, the young man looking for a position in bank or office, viewed the continent as a whole. They sought neither the United States nor Canada, but America and opportunity.

IX

IMMIGRATION AS A FIELD FOR HISTORICAL RESEARCH

THE addition to our population between 1815 and 1914 of thirty-five million Europeans marks an era in American history no less significant than the two centuries of colonization that preceded. In time, the change in sovereignty that occurred in 1776 will be regarded as an unnatural dividing line, and settlement will be viewed as a continuous process from its beginnings in 1607 to its virtual close in 1914. By common usage, however, the term "immigration" applies to the period since the Revolution or, more specifically, to the still later period characterized by individual as distinguished from group migration.

A study of the various waves which have marked high points in the immigrant tide reveals a definite geographic origin for each. The adjectives "old" and "new" are commonly used to describe the change from Northern and Western Europe to the south and east late in the nineteenth century; but this general shift was no more significant than the deviations within each area. At any given time the phenomenon of emigration characterized not a nation as a whole, but a comparatively restricted part of it; and when it again made its appearance, though the participants were still listed as Germans or Italians, their origin was distinct. In every case, the exodus in that district was accompanied by a social and economic reorganization usually indicating an adjustment to modern life. Such reorganizations sometimes took place without emigration to America; but they were always attended by changes in population — perhaps a drift to the cities, perhaps a movement to hitherto waste lands or to other parts of Europe. On occasion they resulted in a congestion of population which produced great social unrest. To the United States the people went only when American industry was prospering, and each wave of migration coincided with an era of unusual business activity. During the century, therefore, it may be said that America was a huge magnet of varying intensity, drawing the people of Europe from those regions where conditions made them mobile and from which transportion provided a path. American conditions determined the duration and height of the waves; European, the particular source.

Accordingly, both Europe and America comprise the field for research. Because students of nineteenth-century Europe have concentrated upon political developments, the student of American immigration will be forced to do much pioneer work which at first glance would seem to have little bearing on his topic. The fact is that emigration has been connected with as many phases of European life as immigration has of American life. Freedom to move, desire to move and means to move summarize these phases. Each requires research, and each is a wide field.

Freedom to move involves the process by which the remaining feudal bonds were loosened and the systems of land tenure revolutionized — in short, that break-up of the solidarity of the community which, in making the individual mobile, forced him to shift for himself. Desire to move concerns political, economic, social and psychological motives, and its roots may be found now in one, now in another, of the great movements of the century. How the emigrant obtained the means to leave is part of the history of the transfer of property and of the development of land and sea transportation.[1]

Until a cheap and safe crossing of the Atlantic was provided, mass emigration was impossible. A study of the emigrant trade from the days when the captain journeyed inland to solicit passengers for his spring voyage to the time when no village was without its agency and no day passed without an emigrant ship leaving some European port would be a contribution to the history of both migration and commerce. But much preliminary work must be done, for the subject is bound up with technical prog-

[1] The student should inquire into topics such as these: the legal development of the right of emigration; military obligations affecting emigration; marriage laws, standards of living and birth and death rates in relation to the growth of population in a given region; migration to cities; division of the common lands; formation of a class of mobile agricultural laborers; laws of tenancy; decline of household industry; changes in systems of land culture; religious movements and ecclesiastical policy; social results of the revolutions of 1848; transport policies of European railroads; effects of competition with American agriculture; effect of crop failures and years of scarcity; popular knowledge of America.

ress, sanitary regulations and the economics of return cargoes.[2]

When upon the high seas, the emigrant was in the hands of some shipping company, and its policies exerted a vital influence on his movements. After the Civil War the rivalries of the lines often proved the dominant factor, as would be shown by a study of the competition of the German and English companies for the control of the Scandinavian trade, or the more general struggle to capture that of the Mediterranean. Rate wars upon the North Atlantic determined the extent and character of American immigration in certain years; and the peace terms which closed these wars had more influence upon the movement in succeeding years than any contemporary American legislation. Moreover, every port of embarkation has its own history, concerned, on the one hand, with the development of its interior net of communications and, on the other, with the nature of its Atlantic commerce. The tobacco trade of Bremen, the cotton trade of Le Havre and the timber trade of Liverpool dictated the American termini of voyages from those ports and thereby determined the racial complexion of certain sections. Were the archives of shipping companies opened, we could see

[2] Some definite subjects will indicate the wide range of interests involved: reasons for the domination of Americans in the trade from 1820 to 1850; effects of the repeal of the British navigation laws in 1849; transfer of shipping to other activities in bringing about a sudden decline, as in 1855; transition, in the carriage of emigrants, from sailing vessels to steamships (1860–1870) in relation to price and to the disappearance of the American flag from the seas.

the agents in operation, and how, when one reservoir of mankind was becoming exhausted, steps were being taken to educate another as to the advantages of emigration.

Though American tariff policy has long been a subject of historical research, the development of the legal conditions under which the most valuable of all our imports has entered has been entirely neglected. The state laws of immigration and settlement are usually characterized as dead letters, but neither the shippers nor the immigrants thought them such. The eventual assumption of regulation by the federal government marked the culmination of a long agitation which concerned the Supreme Court, the transportation companies, organized labor and the farmers. A cross section of these influences could be obtained by studying the Immigration Convention which met at Cincinnati in 1870. The progress of the movement for restriction, leading up to the present-day legislation, involves much social and political history. Castle Garden and Ellis Island are each worthy of a volume; and the administration of laws, the state labor bureaus, and the welfare activities at Boston, Philadelphia, Baltimore, Charleston and New Orleans should not be neglected.

An integral part of the history of immigration is the process of distribution of the newcomers. Just how were the two movements related? Why was it that the periods of small immigration were the periods of most active dispersion? The immediate destination of immigrants during each era of prosperity should be studied, and their participation in the landward movements following the crises in 1819, 1837, 1842, 1857 and 1873 determined. The return European migrations after 1893 and 1907, when it was easier for the immigrant to obtain land in Italy than in America, should receive attention. Not until much detailed research has been done can a theory of distribution be formulated. The investigation of many single aspects will be valuable contributions toward such a theory.

Before the days of the railroad, immigrants considered the journey from the seaport to the interior as difficult as crossing the Atlantic. Often it was as expensive and lasted as long. The immigrant trade on the great natural highways — the Hudson River, the Mississippi, the Ohio and the Great Lakes — should be studied in the same way as that of the Atlantic, in relation to the commerce carried. Pittsburgh and Buffalo, Chicago and St. Louis, should be investigated as immigrant distributing centers. Local ordinances and police restrictions will reveal how the hotels, land offices and labor exchanges were regulated. We should know the reasons for the popularity of certain states or regions at certain times, as Pennsylvania and Illinois in the twenties, Missouri and Ohio in the thirties, Wisconsin in the forties and Iowa and Michigan in the fifties.

With the era of internal improvements a new factor in distribution appears. The census of 1850, the first providing statistics of the foreign-born by counties, reveals all the principal lines of immigrant travel. The zones of settlement represent, in part, accessibility and, in part, the residue left by the construction gangs. An analysis should be made of the labor policy of canals and railroads — the hierarchy of contractors and subcontractors, the recruiting of men, labor conditions and the methods of preserving order. The history of a shanty town may be as rich in primitive self-government as any mining gulch in California.

These alien fringes sometimes resulted from the absconding of the labor contractor; but more often such communities comprised the staff necessary for the upkeep of the canal or railroad, together with those who judiciously chose uncleared lands or snapped up improved farms, and others attracted by the stimulated industrial activity. A study of biographies, in local histories or obituary notices, will reveal how often the nucleus of a later extended foreign settlement began with such pioneers. When the railroads and canals themselves possessed lands, their land policy will explain much settlement. That the great Western railroads rank with the colonial trading companies as American colonizers is becoming recognized, but the influence of the railroads in the older sections should not be overlooked. The opening of the Erie Railroad, for instance, brought thousands of newly arrived immigrants into southern New York and northern Pennsylvania. Access to a market was demanded by the foreigner who settled upon the land, whereas the native American was more self-sufficing.

When the rail net was completed to the Mississippi, the carriage of immigrants became an important feature. This business was sought by the railroads not only for the immediate revenue or the disposal of their lands, but for the more permanent income to be derived from settlement. Hence tickets were sold in the interior villages of Europe, alliances were formed with steamship lines, competition was bitter in the ports, and fares were reduced to ridiculous figures, as in the railroad war of 1885 when for a time the flat rate from New York to Chicago was only a dollar. The varying policies of individual roads, the relation of rates to settlement, the demands of certain industries for the supply of labor, as well as the history of the immigrant train itself as an institution, are all topics worthy of investigation. Nor should the "home seekers' excursions" be forgotten, which in times of industrial depression drew away persons who had settled in congested urban centers.

Land companies and individual landowners supplemented the activities of the railroads. The rise of great land fortunes, the creation of these estates of hundreds of thousands and even millions of acres, is a phase of American settlement as yet obscure. The dissolution of these estates was intimately connected with the immigration of foreigners, as advertisements in the German and English agricultural journals of the seventies and eighties reveal. Agents of such estates were active in European villages, sticking up their posters in public houses, lecturing to improvement clubs and, allied with the railroad and state representatives, smoothing all the difficulties of migration. Though this mode of settlement is most noticeable in the last quarter of the nineteenth century, the same influence operated from the very beginning and often decided the permanent character of a given region. Thus, it was probably the opening of the Astor lands at an opportune moment that turned the tide of Germans to Wisconsin.

But there were also other factors influencing the process of distribution. Religious ties, which must be interpreted as including language and social customs as well as spiritual needs, played an important part. The early history of many rural parishes will show how the minister or priest turned solicitor and, working quietly year after year, changed his feeble missionary charge into a vigorous church. Ecclesiastical administrators undertook comprehensive plans, the Catholic Church producing a group of colonizing bishops in Fenwick of Boston, Ireland of St. Paul and Byrne of Little Rock. The activities of each will repay study. The Irish Colonization Convention, which met at Buffalo in February, 1856, at the suggestion of D'Arcy McGee, proved a failure; but an analysis of the plans there promulgated will prove an interesting indication of racial consciousness, and their final wreck, due to the opposition of Bishop Hughes of New York, will provide an enlightening picture of rival group ambitions. Many congregations, especially of Germans and Scandinavians, migrated as a unit; but although almost any county history of the Middle West mentions the arrival of some such body, the economic history of no one of them has ever been written.

Through the operation of these factors of distribution

the immigrant entered some line of economic activity in country, village or city. His energies usually raised him to a different social plane and, at the same time, influenced the material welfare of his American neighbors. The economic history of foreign farming communities has varied with the local conditions existing upon their arrival and their financial resources.[3] Many immigrants were left stranded in the small towns and villages. Here they served as carpenters, masons, blacksmiths and casual laborers. Some obtained a footing in commercial life and their children became merchants and bankers. Professional men of foreign parentage were recruited almost exclusively from this class, so their influence as leaders of the second generation was far greater than their numerical proportion would warrant. Others of this group, however, were the ne'er-do-wells that have contributed so much to the flavor of Main Street literature.

Industry played a part in the initial stages of dispersion by providing jobs, from the savings of which the immigrant might acquire a farm. Some foreign groups, however, preferred the opportunities and sociability of the cities. The racial evolution of a purely manufacturing

[3] Suggestive subjects for investigation are the immigrant as an outright purchaser; the rise of the hired man to ownership; the immigrant as renter or mortgaged debtor; occupation of abandoned farms by any race; the different racial customs in providing for the second generation; the immigrant as a market gardener, cotton planter or tobacco grower, as a fruitman, rancher or ordinary prairie mixed-farmer; the employment of farm hands and older sons in lumbering, ice cutting and other seasonal labor; the attitude toward improvements and scientific farming.

A FIELD FOR RESEARCH

city, such as Lowell, Massachusetts, will provide illustrations, with the Irish displacing, or at least taking the place of, the Yankees; the French Canadians succeeding the Irish; and they in turn followed by the Greeks and Slavs.[4]

When the process of distribution had been completed and a definite economic status achieved, social life took on clearer form. If the immigrant's lot was cast in a purely American environment, he soon lost his characteristics or became a social hermit. More often, he was surrounded by hundreds who had the same life history and, in company with them, he built up a society neither European nor American. At present there exist probably a score of types of these societies. Research should begin with the effects of the American scene upon the individual. How did it influence his health? When did he discard his old clothing, and when and why did he become ashamed of being "different"? What changes occurred in his principles and morals, and why did he become more ambitious? What new interests did he most easily adopt and which

---

[4] Other topics are immigration in relation to the construction of street railroads, factories, dams and canals, and the dispersion of the workers when completed; the influences which led certain races into certain occupations; the acquisition of city property; rise in the standard of living; levers by which a group raised itself to a higher plane of industry; efforts to retain control of a particular industry against the inroads of later comers; the circumstances that culminated in the anti-contract labor law; attitude of the immigrants to the unions, their radicalism, their conservatism, their leadership, their utilization as strike breakers, and their influence in the formation of the immigrant-restriction laws.

of the old most quickly disappeared? The determination of how immigrant reaction has varied with time, place and nationality may seem to present insuperable difficulties. But it is not impossible. Biographies, reminiscences and letters exist by the thousand; acute observations were made by travelers; and the missionary reports teem with comments.

The social history of the alien family provides a clue to much community development. What variations in internal administration and authority resulted from the migration? The persistence of family traditions, customs and even names, the training of children in the years before going to school, the family pastimes and mutual obligations are pertinent topics. In time the second generation became a disturbing element. Unnumbered household revolutions occurred, the rebels demanding modernization of furniture, food and dress, and often a change of religion. When they succeeded in securing control of the family, the strongest bulwark of hyphenism was carried. The success or failure of such movements should be related to nationality, location, religion and community type.

Finally, community activities demand research. Everyday life in Boston and Milwaukee and a score of other immigrant "capitals" should be described. The sociology of the hundred-and-sixty-acre farm is as worthy of investigation as that of the ante-bellum plantation. What amusements, festivals, commercial and social habits prevailed? How was an immigrant aristocracy created, and was it an expression of European or American standards? What was the opinion as to intermarriage with other groups, and what was the social effect of such alliances? Did each nationality manifest a characteristic attitude toward social problems, such as temperance and Sunday observance? At what stage and why did native prejudice express itself, and did it cause an intensification of peculiarities? What traits persisted after the first generation had passed, and was a constant influx necessary to maintain group individuality?

As long as any community retained its own language, amalgamation with American social life was impossible. From the first, immigrant leaders complained of the eagerness with which the people discarded their mother tongue. Its retention became the cornerstone of all efforts to maintain solidarity. Historically, therefore, the problem has two aspects: first, the varying circumstances that led to the adoption of English; and, secondly, the positive language-policy of the leaders. The matter being so personal, the materials for the study of the first are scant. But the second generation, now so widely represented in the colleges, might be subjected to a questionnaire, for it was in the inner life of the bilingual families that the transition took place. For the second point the materials are abundant. Sooner or later in every denomination the language question arose, and the proceedings of church conventions and the columns of the official organs are filled with debates and resolutions. Even more abundant are the materials for a history of the teaching of foreign languages in the public schools. Every state board of education was subjected to tremendous pressure, and in many states every ward and school district witnessed similar propaganda. The language legislation during the World War, interesting as a manifestation of war psychology, can be more clearly understood in the light of these concessions.

But the language question is but one phase of the much broader subject of the migration of institutions. How these institutions were set up, how they throve in the American atmosphere, and how they competed with the native institutions form part of the history of immigration. The process of their transplantation is obscure, though a few years after settlement we can see them in full bloom — churches, parochial schools, academies, fraternal organizations.[5] There are Portuguese bands, Welsh eisteddfods, German turnvereins, Bohemian sokols and Polish falcons.[6] Each nationality at every period demands special study.

[5] There were other parts of the world to which emigrating Europeans took their institutions. As many Irish settled in England in the years after the famine as in America; Italians by the hundreds of thousands colonized the Argentine; and there are flourishing German settlements in Brazil. By comparing the institutional history of these groups in the differing environments, the problems and significance of their development in the United States may be the more clearly understood.

[6] In connection with their origin many questions arise. Did the immigrants create these institutions because they could join no others, or because they were content only with their own? Did these institutions arise spontaneously, or were they due to the activity of enterprising individuals? Was assistance in finance or leadership received from any society in the home country and, if so, what were the motives of this society?

A FIELD FOR RESEARCH

What applies to the Irish differs from what applies to the Hungarians; and conditions among the Germans in 1840 are different from those in 1880. The situation varies with the intensity of national feeling in the European countries, with the amount of support given by organizations at home, with the internal politics of the immigrant group in America, and with the amount of opposition which native institutions exhibited.

It was the American churches and their missionary activities that offered the strongest resistance. They met the invaders on their own ground and fought them with their own language. Maintaining seminaries on American soil, they had an advantage which the European training schools could not duplicate, and their success was the despair of the early missionaries from the churches of Europe. Psychologically, the years of migration provided a fertile field for the propagation of new faiths, and the result was the division of the nationalities, especially the old immigrants, among sects and the breakup of migrating denominations into many branches. Much as these divisions were to be deplored from the point of view of effective religious service, they did act as agents of Americanization by dissolving the ties with European hierarchies and placing administration in the hands of those who were directed by American organizations.[7]

---

[7] The problem of the organization of immigrants may be approached through biography. A few among the hundreds of such pioneers are the Catholics, James Fitton and Henry Lemcke; the

This mingling of social systems raises the natural question: what has immigration as a whole, or any national stock, contributed to American culture? Many intellectuals among the newcomers thought of themselves as the bearers of a higher civilization, and their descendants have been assiduous in pressing these claims, so that today the national origin of every man who achieved distinction has been duly acclaimed. We have lists of statesmen, soldiers, poets, novelists, engineers and educators, presenting a formidable array. But this method does not reach the heart of the problem. It is in the township, the village or the city ward that the leaven in the lump can be detected. There the investigator will find the German singing society, which gradually took into its ranks non-Germans, stimulated the formation of other organizations and provided a winter's concert course. There he will find the immigrant music teacher, who passed on the training of his Old World masters to the offspring of a dozen nations. He will see a reading circle develop into a library reflecting the particular bent of its originators, thereby helping to determine the literary character of the community. He will see the immigrant schoolmaster transmitting his own training and producing among his pupils an unusually large proportion of scientists, philosophers or farmers. When a few hundred such studies have been made and compared, we can more

---

Lutherans, C. F. W. Walther and L. P. Esbjørn; the Methodist, Wilhelm Nast; and the two Protestant Episcopal bishops, Philander Chase and Jackson Kemper.

confidently say what each group has contributed to the cultural possessions of American society.

In certain centers the mingling of immigrant contributions may be analyzed. There are the universities, many of whose professors have been drawn from European institutions, and whose training is reflected in the organization and scope of the curriculum. Hundreds of each nationality have sat in Congress and in the state legislatures. Have they been conspicuous in producing legislation to foster the arts and sciences? In the cities theaters have been promoted by almost every alien group. When they disappeared, did they leave any trace of their influence upon the American stage? At what times and for what reasons have European classics become popular, either in the original or in translation? What scientific, literary, artistic or musical causes have been championed by the foreign groups? What literature did the immigrants beget, and what characteristic traits of American literature derive from such origins? [8]

These questions can be answered only by access to sources that depict the inner life of a group. Such a source

---

[8] The immigrants produced many novelists whose work will never live as belles-lettres, but as reactions to American environment these attempts repay study. Characters and plots are drawn from the community life with which the authors were acquainted. Mrs. Mary Sadlier and Paul Peppergrass (John Boyce) write of the Irish, J. R. Psenka of the Czechs, and Abraham Cahan of the Russian Jews. Among the Scandinavian writers are the well-known Knut Hamsun and Johan Bojer. But less prominent authors such as the Norwegian, Waldemar Ager, should not be overlooked.

is the widespread foreign-language press.[9] To peruse its pages gives a vivid cross section of community activities. But it is as a political exponent or political instructor that the immigrant press merits the greatest attention. With the increasing percentage of naturalized voters, its relation to the succeeding political crises becomes of greater significance. In another and increasingly important field it became the guide — foreign affairs. Whatever may be said of the course of the American press generally in respect to European news before the World War, the foreign-language newspapers were not ignorant, and did not slight such topics. Each of the diplomatic crises that mark the advance to August, 1914, forms the basis of news and editorial comment that reflected prevailing opinion in the country of origin. Consequently, these people in America were almost as prepared for war, psychologically, as any in Europe; and when the conflict did come, the whole battery of the press was turned upon the American policy of neutrality, thus creating many of the internal problems of the troubled years from 1914 to 1917. The historian who attempts to unravel the political skein of that

[9] In addition to a study of certain papers which may be called the mouthpieces of their respective groups, it would be enlightening to investigate the careers of the leading journalists. Among them are Oswald Ottendorfer of the New York *Staats-Zeitung*, Hermann Raster of the *Illinois Staats-Zeitung*, William Doenzer of the *Anzeiger des Westens*, John Anderson of the *Skandinaven*, Byrnild Anundsen of the *Decorah Posten*, Patrick Donahoe and John B. O'Reilly of the *Boston Pilot*, Patrick Ford of the *Irish World*, James A. McMaster of the New York *Freeman's Journal*, Hans Mattson of the *Svenska Amerikaner* and Solon J. Vlastos of the Greek paper *Atlantis*.

period must first trace the development of the international state of mind of these groups.

In the formation of this state of mind the press was by 1914 receiving the assistance of powerful allies. The foreign elements were becoming more conscious of their origin. Immigrants of forty years' residence were becoming reflective. An unusually large number of reminiscences appeared; histories were being written; and alliances, foundations and leagues were being organized. Though largely cultural in their ambitions, these societies could not exclude politics in times of crisis, and in 1914 they played the rôle in national politics which for practically a century local societies had enacted in their own neighborhoods.

It is in these local circles that the student of the political influence of immigrant groups will make his start. There are perhaps a hundred such clubs that demand a historian. He will investigate the circumstances attending the organization of each, trace the political allegiance of the moving spirits in the venture, analyze its program, ferret out the speakers, and interpret the toasts at the annual banquets. Soon he will find its leaders becoming aldermen and its more prosperous members being favored with city and state contracts. The advantages of naturalization are urged, and committees appointed to welcome the immigrants and train them in the political way in which they should go. These features, be it emphasized, are not necessarily the most important activities of the society; but this approach to the problem is the direct path into the maze of local politics, where new and bewildered voters are captured for this or that party, and in turn the party is influenced in its attitude toward public issues.

The immigrant came with preconceived attitudes which conditioned his reaction to American life. One of them relates that for ten years before his departure he read all the letters which reached the village from those who had already migrated; and when he heard that here or there within the range of a dozen miles someone had returned to visit relatives or friends, he called on foot to catechize him more particularly. From such reminiscences, in newspapers, magazines and books, an attempt should be made to deduce the prevailing attitude toward American problems at various periods, in order to estimate the background of political reactions. Important among such sources are the addresses and writings of the many successful immigrants who later returned to their native country to serve as ministers and consuls.

The political machines found the alien voters susceptible. The issues that were emphasized, the attentions paid to visiting foreign notables, the injection of religious controversies, were all means to an end. The fire, police and street departments of every city have an immigrant history. Naturalization clubs flourished in all large communities, some of them bona-fide efforts to train immigrants to become citizens, others the creatures of the machine. As early as the decade of the thirties, efforts to secure the German or Irish vote may be recognized locally. The spread of such tactics from city government to state government and thence into national politics should be traced.

In the rural regions the foreigners in a township were either so few that they did not count, or so many that they had entire control. A township of the latter type provides an enlightening laboratory. Here is a community governed by men who perhaps had no training in democracy. Under such circumstances what type of men came forward? Did they merely imitate their neighbors, or were they more progressive or more conservative? To which did they pay the more attention, schools or roads? Were the German immigrants after 1848 more politically minded than their predecessors, and did any change occur after 1871? It is questions such as these that the student who has before him the records of a North Dakota or a Wisconsin township can answer.

With these matters disposed of, it will be more possible to generalize as to whether the immigrants have contributed anything to American political ideals.[10] Perhaps they retarded the progress of democracy by burdening it with a mass of citizens unprepared for self-government. It may be that their European attitude led to more social legislation and fostered the movement toward centralization. On occasion, they have been more interested in

[10] Political biography offers a great array of governors and members of Congress. They should be studied with particular reference to the group from which they came. Governor John A. Johnson, Senators Knute Nelson and James Shields, and the Bohemian, Charles Jonas, who had a varied career at home and abroad, are cases in point.

fighting the battles of the old country than in participating in the affairs of the new.[11] Irish, German, Hungarian, Polish and Italian patriotic movements operated from an American base about the middle of the last century; and research will probably reveal that the emergence of the new nations of Eastern and Central Europe in consequence of the World War was possible only because there had existed in America, for a generation or two, active colonies of those nationalities, which had kept alive the ideal of independence and could offer financial support and political pressure at the critical moment. Such activities, which to the natives seemed alien to American life, prepared the way for the antiforeigner movements from the time of the Know Nothings down to the era of the present immigration act.

Countries of origin were dismayed by their loss when they saw their ports thronged with the sturdiest of their peasantry. Efforts to stem the movement were attempted. Special attention should be directed to the Scandinavian societies which agitated against emigration, and the relation of empire settlement to variations in the flow of the British current. The positive policy of Italy in securing economic advantages from the movement will be found an essential factor in the development of the characteristics of the "new" immigration.

---

[11] This is especially true of the Irish, who for almost a century championed the cause of their island through a series of movements: the Repeal agitation of the forties, the Fenianism of the sixties, the Land League of the eighties, and the Sinn Fein movement of the early twentieth century.

European governments, moreover, realized that their political as well as their economic life was involved. Experience with a few returned radicals revealed a new threat to their institutions. Consequently, persons who had been in America were regarded with suspicion and, if necessary, their freedom in action and speech was limited. At times newspapers, periodicals, books and even personal letters were subjected to censorship. Here is a rich field for those who would trace the development of nineteenth-century democracy. What influence American political theory had upon the minds of those who were the leaders; how the framework of the American republic was the model for projected European republics; and how the peasant who had neither political theories nor visionary governments in mind began vaguely to feel that things could be better because they were better across the Atlantic — these matters require investigation.

The source material from which the history of immigration can be drawn is infinite. Not until the movement was clearly defined were bureaus for its supervision created by the European governments. Long before their reports appear, however, pertinent official documents are available. There are ponderous investigations of land tenure, feudal services, taxation, marriage laws, poverty and military affairs. Petitions to legislatures provoked debates in which members gave testimony and suggested remedies. Consuls residing abroad reported on the fate of fellow countrymen who had settled in their districts.

Charitable organizations investigated the feasibility of obtaining relief by systematic emigration and, in doing so, laid bare the social maladjustments that were stimulating departure. Farmers discussed the problem of rural labor at their meetings, and local correspondents of agricultural journals commented on the changes in population that were effecting a revolution in local society.

In the countries of Northwest Europe, emigration produced a literature of its own. Before commerce undertook the task of watching over the voyager from his native village to his new home, emigrants traveled "by the book." A comparative study of these guidebooks reveals the changes that took place from decade to decade in the routes, difficulties, costs and even motives of emigration. The files of emigrants' periodicals also present a rich opportunity, with their advertisements of land and transportation companies, news items, letters from settlers, notes on labor conditions, and descriptive poetry and fiction.[12]

---

[12] The following list of German and Swiss emigrant papers indicates their nature: *Der Nordamerikaner* (St. Gall, 1833–1834); *Allgemeine Auswanderungs-Zeitung* (Rudolstadt, 1846–1871); *Der Deutsche Auswanderer* (Darmstadt, 1847–1850); *Germania, Archiv zur Kenntniss des Deutschen Elements in allen Ländern der Erde* (Frankfurt am Main, 1847–1850); *Der Sächsische Auswanderer* (Leipzig, 1848–1851); *Der Auswanderer am Niederrhein* (Meurs, 1848–1849), a series of pamphlets; *Deutsche Auswanderer-Zeitung* (Bremen, 1852–1875); *Hansa, Central Organ für Deutsche Auswanderung* (Hamburg, 1852–1857); *Hamburger Zeitung für Deutsche Auswanderungs- und Kolonisations-Angelegenheiten* (Hamburg, 1852–1858); *Das Westland: Magazin zur Kunde Amerikanischer Verhältnisse* (Bremen, 1851–1852); *Atlantis: Zeitschrift für Leben und Literatur in England und Amerika* (Dessau,

A FIELD FOR RESEARCH

In time, the business of catering to the needs of emigrants became a major concern of the ports of embarkation. Their newspapers and commercial journals and the official city and port documents report the almost daily variation in the flow as well as the general trade conditions influencing transportation. City information bureaus were established, protective societies formed, and religious organizations were not slow in undertaking mission-

---

1853–1854); *Neuestes über Auswanderung und von Ausgewanderten* (1850–1853), an annual review edited by August Schultze; *Anschauungen und Erfahrungen in Nordamerika, eine Monatschrift* (Zurich, 1853–1855); *Schilderungen aus Amerika, eine Monatschrift* (Zurich, 1859–1860); *Taschen-Bibliothek der Reise-, Zeit-, und Lebensbilder* (Rudolstadt, 1854–1857), including an annual emigrants' calendar; *Der Tollense-Bote, Blätter zur Unterhaltung und Belehrung, Auswanderungs-Zeitung und Anzeiger für Mecklenburg* (Neubrandenburg, 1855–1856); *Der Emigrant* (Bremen, 1868); *Der Auswanderer* (Zurich, 1872–1873); *Der Pfadfinder* (Gotha, 1872–1873); *Weltpost: Blätter für Deutsche Auswanderung, Kolonisation, und Weltverkehr* (Leipzig, 1881–1885); *Neue Auswanderungs-Zeitung* (Leipzig, 1880–1881), continued as *Deutsch-Amerikanische Zeitung* (1882); and *Amerikanische Nachrichten* (Berlin, 1883–1884), continued as *Deutsche Weltpost* (1885–1886). In addition to these, the third volume of *Der Kolonist* (Bern) appeared in 1854, and the eighth volume of the *Schweizerische Auswanderungszeitung* (Bern), in 1873; but I have not yet been able to locate complete files of these two papers. For British emigrants the following papers, all published in London, appeared: *Emigration Gazette* (1841–1843); *Emigrant and Colonial Gazette* (1848–1849); *Sidney's Emigrant's Journal* (1848–1849); *Universal Emigration and Colonial Messenger* (1850–1851); *Emigration Record and Colonial Journal* (1856–1858); *Land and Emigration* (1871–1873); and *American Settler* (1872–1874 and 1880–1892). The *Anglo-American Times* (1865–1896), though not primarily an emigrant journal, contains a great deal of information about land, the process of settlement and the industrial situation. For other useful newspapers, see the bibliography of M. L. Hansen, *The Atlantic Migration* (Cambridge, 1940).

ary work. All these left records. The actual transatlantic journey is depicted in the works of travelers, most of whom inspected the steerage. The less picturesque aspects of the traffic may be discovered in the annual reports of shipping companies, the columns of commercial periodicals and the findings of official investigations.

In America all sources of pioneer history can make a contribution, but there are two which bear directly on the foreign elements. One is the immigrant press discussed above, the other the great mass of literature connected with the religious condition of the immigrants. Bishops and missionaries on their travels could not overlook the material situation of their flocks, and in their reports this interest is reflected. How much lies buried in church archives can only be imagined; the great amount that found its way into print has hardly been touched.[13] In Europe societies were formed to promote the spiritual welfare of the emigrants, and their publications are even more informative.[14]

But such materials can be found in few libraries to

[13] How extensive this literature is may be realized by referring to the article "Periodical Literature" in the *Catholic Encyclopedia*, XI, 692–696, and the list of Lutheran papers in J. G. Morris, *Bibliotheca Lutherana* (Phila., 1876), 131–139.

[14] The most important of these publications are *Annales de l'association de la propagation de la foi* (Lyons, 1827–   ); *Berichte der Leopoldinen-Stiftung im Kaiserthum Oesterreich* (Vienna, 1832–   ); *Das Missionsblatt* (Barmen, 1826–   ); *Allgemeine Zeitung des Judenthums* (Leipzig, 1837–   ); *Kirchliche Mitteilungen aus und über Nordamerika* (Berlin, 1843–   ); *Missionsblatt der Brüdergemeinde* (Hamburg, 1837–   ); and *Fliegende Blätter aus dem Rauhen Hauses zu Horn* (Hamburg, 1844–   ).

which students have ready access. A painstaking search is necessary before the investigator can attack his problems. Accordingly, it is suggested that, as the first step in developing the field, a survey be made to locate the raw materials. Such a survey would extend beyond the libraries of universities and the great public libraries. It would explore the riches of the theological institutions and the archives of church headquarters. It would reveal unexpected treasures on the shelves of local historical societies and in the libraries of immigrant communities. Such a comprehensive investigation would do more than shorten the labors of the student. It would be the best guarantee that the history of American immigration will be written on the broad and impartial lines that its place in our national development deserves.

INDEX

Abolition, and Puritanism, 99
Acadians, expulsion of, 178
Africa, migration to, 5, 21
Ager, Waldemar, as author, 207 *n*.
Agrarianism, the immigrant influences, 94–95
Agriculture, as factor in immigration, 19, 21–23; the immigrant influences, 22; pioneer, 62–64; New England, 160, 161, 166, 171–172; Civil War affects, 167–168; Canadian, 181. *See also* Agrarianism, Farmers, Land
American Federation of Labor, conservatism of, 90
American Home Missionary Society, subsidizes pastors, 119–120
Amusements, on shipboard, 40, 51; Puritan, 104; Scandinavian Sabbath, 117; banned, 120; in Virginia, 125; German, 134; as field for research, 202
Anarchism, the immigrant and, 87–89
Anundsen, Byrnild, as journalist, 208 *n*.
Arbeiter Zeitung, and labor movement, 88
Argentina, migration to, 6, 21; Italians in, 204 *n*.
Australia, migration to, 5, 21, 23, 24–25

Baltimore, subjects for research in, 195

Banking and finance, internationalized, 7–8
Belfast, migration from, 6
Birkbeck settlement, 22
Bjørnson, Bjørnstjerne, visits America, 144
Blue Laws, practical aspect of, 104
Bohemians, in politics, 93; as Catholics, 146
Bojer, Johan, as author, 207 *n*.
Boston, as intellectual center, 98; intemperance, 106; tolerance, 106–107; immigrant labor in, 154–155; immigrant trade, 156–157; Germans in, 166; subjects for research in, 195, 202
Boyce, John, as author, 207 *n*.
Brazil, migration to, 20–21; Germans in, 204 *n*.
Bremen, immigrant trade, 6, 31; tobacco trade, 194
British Columbia, migration to, 182, 186
Buffalo, as immigrant distributing center, 196; Irish Colonization Convention at, 199

Cahan, Abraham, as author, 207 *n*.
California, Puritanism in, 104; migration to, 182, 187
Canada, extent of nineteenth-century immigration to, 21; Company induces settlement, 22–23; Fenians attack, 143; French leave, 154, 170, 187–188; Irish

migrate to, 158-159; timber trade of, 160; nature of migration across border of, 175-176, 184-185; statistics of migration from, 176, 184; early American migration to, 178-179; relation of westward movement to migration to, 180-181, 186-187; Great Britain colonizes, 181; causes of migration from, 181-183; efforts to develop, 184; railroads promote settlement or, 184-186; twentieth century migration to, 186; encourages "repatriation," 189

Canadian Pacific Railroad, speeds settlement, 185-186

Canadians, American colonies of, 181-182; in the Civil War, 183; in U. S. in 1890, 184; U. S. hospitality to, 184-185. *See also* French Canadians

Cape Cod, Portuguese on, 172-173

Capitalism, and the Constitution, 84; immigrant attitude toward, 85, 95

Carnegie, Andrew, mentioned, 150

Castle Garden, as subject for research, 195

Catholic Church, tolerance toward, 107; fights intemperance, 110, 122-123; movement against, 111; colonizing activities of, 121, 199; retards Puritanism, 122; language problem in, 146-147; in Maine, 159

Census, *see* U. S. census

Charleston, subjects for research in, 195

Chicago, labor movement in, 87-88; as immigrant distributing center, 196

Children, on shipboard, 39, 41; effort to prevent Americanizing of, 120; education of, 134, 140

Chinese, in New England, 169-170

Churches, Haymarket affair stirs immigrant, 89; immigration discouraged by Continental, 114-115; German dislike of American, 134; cultural development and, 136-137, 144; in Cincinnati, 140; language in, 145-147. *See also* Catholic Church, Religion

Cincinnati, Germans in, 139, 140; Immigration Convention at, 195

Civil War, relation of expansion to, 54; Puritanism and, 99; affects immigrant cultural development, 140; improves immigrant economic status, 141, 150; the immigrant in, 141-143; results of, 167-168, 183-184, 188; Canadians in, 183

Colleges and universities, established, 101, 120; immigrant contribution to, 207

Colonizing schemes, German, 131-133

Commerce, *see* Trade

Communistic societies, in America, 86; immigrant attitude toward, 87

Congress, protects women on shipboard, 40; refuses land grants, 132; immigrants in, 207, 211 *n*.

Connecticut, temperance in, 105; Irish in, 155; Germans in, 166

INDEX

Constitution, American pride in, 78; capitalism and, 84; Shays's Rebellion and, 85
Cooking, on shipboard, 35–37
Corn laws, affect Irish, 162
Corporations, created, 55; and railroad development, 76
Cotton trade, aids immigration, 157, 194
Crime, on shipboard, 42; and Puritanism, 103–104
Cromwell, Oliver, sends Scots to New England, 154
Cudahy, Michael, mentioned, 150
Cunard, Samuel, aids migration, 6

Democracy, free land preserves, 57; immigrants seek, 78–82; stability of American, 83–85; the immigrant influences, 95–96, 211
Democratic party, the immigrant in, 95; and Know Nothings, 136
Depression, relation of frontier to, 58; relation of westward movement to, 69; strengthens Puritanism, 112; of 1893, 150
Diet, *see* Food
Doenzer, William, as journalist, 208 *n.*
Donahoe, Patrick, as journalist, 208 *n.*
Draft law, immigrant attitude toward, 141–142
Drama, in Boston, 106–107; immigrant contribution to, 139, 140
Drunkenness, prevalent, 106; immigrant, 109–110, 113–115
Dutch, in New York, 124; in Berkshires, 154; Americanized, 155

Education, on shipboard, 41; frontier theory of, 58–59; Puritanism in, 101; religious, 120; Germans deplore American, 134; parochial, 140, 205; foreign-language, 203–204; immigrant contribution to, 206, 207
Ellis Island, as subject for research, 195
Emerson, R. W., as author, 98
Emigrants, *see* Immigrants
Emigration, *see* Immigration
England, increased migration from, 147–148, 168; Irish in, 204 *n.*
Englishmen, as American pioneers, 73; in American intellectual life, 130, 147–149; in industrial New England, 168–169
Erie Railroad, speeds settlement, 197
Expansion, keynote of American development, 54–65. *See also* Frontier, Homestead law, Westward movement

Fall River, manufacturing in, 168–169
Famine, causes migration, 162
Farmer-Labor party, the immigrant in, 94
Farmers, pioneer, 62–65; immigrants as, 65–76; Germans as, 151, 154–155; Irish as, 161, 165; Jews as, 173
Farmers' Nonpartisan League, formed, 94
Fenian movement, 143, 212 *n.*
Fine arts, immigrant contribution to, 138–139, 153; of second col-

onization, 173–174. *See also* arts by name
Finns, in New England, 173
Fishing, off Newfoundland Banks, 49
Food, on shipboard, 36–37, 48–49; American, 145; Italian, 152
Ford, Patrick, as journalist, 208 *n.*
Forty-eighters, their rôle in America, 134–135
Fourier, F. M. C., communities of, 86
France, war with, 105, 179; Italians in, 151–152; Huguenots flee, 154. *See also* Le Havre
French Canadians, in New England, 154, 170, 188–189, 201; in the West, 187; return to Canada, 189
French Line, attracts immigrants, 6–7
Frontier, theory formulated, 56–59; and Puritanism, 104. *See also* Homestead law, Westward movement

Germans, migrate to Brazil, 20, 24, 204 *n.*; newspapers of, 28; prepare to migrate, 30–31, 33; on shipboard, 36; as farmers, 61–62, 67, 73, 151, 154–155; in Pennsylvania, 87, 125; in labor movement, 87–89; in politics, 90–91, 93, 148, 210–211; as Catholics, 121; as intellectuals, 131; colonizing schemes of, 131–133; preserve social institutions, 133–134; growth of nationalism among, 135–136; cultural development of, 136–140, 144, 206; in Civil War, 142; in the churches, 146, 147; in New England, 154–155, 166; Americanized, 155–156; migrate after Civil War, 168; in Wisconsin, 199; field for research in congregations of, 199; in patriotic movements, 212
Germany, emigrant trade of, 6, 31, 38, 157; colonial expansion of, 8–9; reasons for migration from, 79–80; Italians in, 151–152
Giles, Henry, quoted, 174
Glasgow, migration from, 6
Gompers, Samuel, in labor movement, 90
Great Britain, colonial expansion of, 8; migration from, 21–23; colonizes Canada, 181. *See also* England
Great Lakes, immigrant trade, 196
Greeks, in industry, 173, 201
Guidebooks, influence of, 19, 45; on pioneering, 66; as material for research, 214

Halifax, migration via, 178
Hamburg, migration from, 24, 31
Hamburg-American Line, organized, 6
Hamsun, Knut, on Americans, 60, 149; on ministers, 121 *n.*
Harriott, John, quoted, 106
Harvard University, influence of, 120
Hasselquist, T. N., as clergyman, 116 *n.*, 120 *n.*
Hawthorne, Nathaniel, as author, 98
Haymarket riot, 88

Health, on shipboard, 34, 44; on the frontier, 60; famine impairs, 162; of New England impaired, 171

Historians, immigrants as, 25–26, 28; sociologists as, 26; professional, 26–28; of frontier theory, 56–59

Homestead law, and the immigrant, 72–76, 145; speeds settlement, 183–184

Hudson River immigrant trade, 196

Hughes, Bishop, opposes Irish Colonization Convention, 199

Huguenots, flee to New England, 154; Americanized, 155

Hungarians, in patriotic movements, 212

Illinois, English in, 22; immigrant farmers in, 67; Irish in, 165; colonized, 181, 196; French Canadians in, 187

Immigrants, prepare to migrate, 30–33, 129; set sail, 34; on shipboard, 35–51; reach America, 50–52; as frontiersmen, 65–67; as farmers, 67–76; as homesteaders, 72–76; as democrats, 82; second-generation, 83, 93–95, 145, 150, 202; in labor movement, 87–90; in politics, 90–96; immorality among, 113–115; puritanized, 116–121; as journalists, 137–138; in the fine arts, 138–139; in Civil War, 141–143. *See also* nationalities by name

Immigration, influences building of U. S., 9–11; influences social evolution, 11–13, 16; historians of, 25–29; preparations for, 30–33, 129; influences westward movement, 65–76; by families, 68–71; reasons for, 77–82, 130; efforts to curb, 79, 111, 114–115, 212; and Puritanism, 101–104, 108–111; increases after Civil War, 127, 142, 148, 168; "new," 150–153; trade facilitates, 157–160; Convention at Cincinnati, 195. *See also* countries and nationalities by name

Imperialism, growth of, 8–9

Indiana, the immigrant in, 22; colonized, 181

Industry, relation of migration to, 4, 5–6, 69, 177, 192; on shipboard, 39, 41; American expansion of, 55; the immigrant in American, 69, 150; lumber, 75; New England, 107–108, 154–155, 166, 168–170; Irish in, 108, 160–161, 163–165, 201; Civil War affects, 150, 167–168, 183; Italians in, 152–153; Germans in, 154–155, 166; English in, 168–169; Chinese in, 169–170; British Canadians in, 183; French Canadians in, 188, 201; as field for research, 197, 200–201

Intellectual life, *see* Drama, Education, Journalism, Lawyers, Literature

Iowa, immigrant farmers in, 67; immigrant political influence in, 90–91; Norwegians in, 144; migration from Canada to, 182; popularity of, 196

Ireland, population changes in,

18; preparations for leaving, 31; sailing from, 37; trade promotes migration from, 158–159; famine causes migration from, 162

Irish, prepare to migrate, 31; as farmers, 67, 161, 165; labor in New England, 108–111, 160–161, 163–164, 201; as intellectuals, 130; seek land grants, 132; growth of nationalism among, 135–136; in Civil War, 142, 143; in patriotic movements, 143, 212 *n.*; priests, 146; in colonial New England, 154; Americanized, 156; trade promotes migration of, 156–159; characterized, 161–162, 164; in New England, 204 *n.*; in politics, 210–211

Irish Colonization Convention, at Buffalo, 199

Italian Line, organized, 6

Italians, as Catholics, 146; contributions of, 151–153; in New England, 173; in the Argentine, 204 *n.*; in patriotic movements, 212

Italy, migration to, 196, 212

Jews, in New England, 173

Johns Hopkins University, Turner at, 56–57

Johnson, J. A., as subject for study, 211 *n.*

Jonas, Charles, as subject for study, 211 *n.*

Journalism, immigrant, 137–138. *See also* Newspapers

Kansas, the immigrant in, 90–91

Know-Nothing movement, and Puritanism, 111–112; strengthens nationalistic feeling, 136; Civil War affects, 167

Labor movement, the immigrant in, 87–90; as field for research, 201 *n.*

La Follette, R. M., as governor, 92–93

Land, policy of Canada, 22–23, 184; speculation, 60; grants, 76, 132; League, 143; in Italy, 196; companies, 198. *See also* Agriculture, Frontier, Homestead law

Language, studied on shipboard, 41; difficulties in America, 131; use of German, 133–134; teaching of German, 140; Norwegian, 82–83, 144; increased use of English, 145, 147–149; the church and, 146–147, 203; question as field for research, 203–204

Latin America, migration to, 19–21; Italians in, 152

Lawyers, immigrants as, 130, 131

Legislation, abroad checks immigration, 17; expansion affects, 55; frontier theory affects, 59; reflects Puritanism, 100, 104; liquor, 111–112; Sabbath, 124; regarding paupers, 157, 162; federal immigration, 173, 195; as subject for research, 195; language, 204

Le Havre, migration from, 31, 37–38; cotton trade, 194

Letters, influence of, 19, 70–71, 210; as source of information,

INDEX

41; on pioneering, 66; on drinking, 109, 115; as research material, 202; censored, 213
Libraries, the immigrant and, 139, 206
Lincoln, Abraham, studies German, 148
Literature, Puritanism in, 97–98; liberalism in, 107; immigrant influence in, 138, 206, 207; of second colonization, 173–174; as field for research, 207
Liverpool, migration from, 6, 31, 37, 47; timber trade, 194
Living conditions, of immigrants, 69, 108, 151
Longfellow, H. W., as author, 98
Lowell, Mass., the immigrant in, 201
Lowell, J. R., as author, 98
Loyalists, as pioneers, 179
Lumber industry, the immigrant and, 75
Lutheran Church, discipline in, 118–119; language of, 147

McGee, D'Arcy, and Irish Colonization Convention, 199
McMaster, J. A., as journalist, 208 *n.*
Maine, prohibition in, 111; Germans in, 155; Irish in, 159; migration to, 179
Manufacturing, the immigrant in, 163–164, 167, 168–170, 173
Maryland, orthodoxy in, 124, 125
Massachusetts, intolerance, 124; agriculture, 161; Chinese in, 169–170; manufacturing in, 201. *See also* Boston

Materials for research: newspapers and periodicals, 28, 207–209, 214–216; ordinances and police regulations, 196; biographies, 197, 202, 205 *n.*, 211 *n.*; obituary notices, 197; letters, 202; missionary reports, 202; proceedings of church conventions, 203; novels, 207 *n.*; reminiscences, 210; official documents, 213; guidebooks, 214; travelers' accounts, 216; shipping-company reports, 216
Mattson, Hans, as journalist, 208 *n.*
Medicine, the immigrant in, 130, 131
Michigan, migration to, 176, 182, 187, 196
Migrations, early, 3, 13–16; statistics of, 4; rules controlling, 4–5; affect industry, 5–6; affect trade, 6–8; affect imperialism, 8–9; nineteenth-century, 18–25; reasons for, 19; to and from Canada, 175–190. *See also* Immigration
Milwaukee, immigrants in, 28, 139, 142; subjects for research in, 202
Minnesota, immigrant farmers in, 67; immigrant political influence in, 94; Norwegians in, 144
Mississippi River immigrant trade, 196
Mississippi Valley, English in, 147–148
Missouri, immigrant farmers in, 67; popularity of, 196
Music, the immigrant and, 137, 139–140, 206

INDEX

National origins, determined, 10; provision, 17

Nationalism, growth of immigrant, 135–136

Naturalization, immigrants seek, 78; efforts to hinder, 111; increased, 208; urged, 209; clubs, 210

Nebraska, immigrant political influence in, 90–91

Nelson, Knute, in politics, 91–92; as subject for study, 211 *n*.

New Brunswick, timber trade, 157; migration from, 182

New Deal, relation of frontier theory to, 59

New England, Puritanism, 97–107; industrialized, 107–108; Irish in, 108–111, 160–167; religious education in, 120; first colonization of, 154–155; first Americanization of, 155–156; Canadian trade promotes second colonization of, 156–160; industry, 160–161, 163–164, 168–170; agriculture, 161, 166, 171–172; Germans in, 166–167; English in, 168–169; Chinese in, 169–170; French in, 170; varied composition of, 172–173; legislation ends second colonization of, 173; migration from, 177–179, 180; French Canadians in, 188–189

New Harmony community, 22

New Haven, orthodoxy in, 124

New Jersey, Puritanism in, 124–125; migration from, 178–179

New Netherland, Sabbath observance in, 124

New Orleans, subjects for research in, 195

New York, immigrant farmers in, 67; Dutch in, 124; migration from, 180

New York City, petitions Congress, 40; Irish in, 132, 142; Bjørnson in, 144; passenger rates to, 158–159

New Zealand, migration to, 21, 23

Newfoundland Banks, fishing at, 49; migration via, 178

Newspapers, as material for research, 28, 208; German, 28, 140, 148; on shipboard, 42; and labor movement, 88–89; criticize Scandinavians, 117; reflect Americanization, 137–138; World War in foreign-language, 208–209; censored, 213

North Dakota, immigrant political influence in, 90–91, 94; materials for research in, 211

North German Lloyd, organized, 6

Norwegians, journals of, 28; perpetuate language, 82–83; in Wisconsin, 114 *n*.; churches of, 144; immigrate after Civil War, 168

Ocean Monarch, burned, 46

Ohio, the immigrant in, 67, 165; popularity of, 196

Ohio River immigrant trade, 196

Olson, F. B., as governor, 94

Oregon, migration to, 187

O'Reilly, J. B., as journalist, 208 *n*.

Ottendorfer, Oswald, as journalist, 208 *n*.

Owen, Robert, communities of, 22, 86

Painting, immigrant contribution to, 139
Panic of 1857, strengthens Puritanism, 112; affects immigrants, 141
Paris, German migration via, 31
Pauperism, immigrant, 108, 110–111, 162
Pennsylvania, immigrants in, 67, 87, 124–125; Puritanism in, 124–125; migration from, 178–179; popularity of, 196
People's party, rise of, 90; the immigrant and, 90–91
Periodicals, opportunities for research in, 214–216
Peru, migration to, 21
Philadelphia, Irish in, 132; materials for research in, 195
Physical culture, German, 139–140
Pittsburgh, as immigrant distributing center, 196
Poles, as Catholics, 146; in patriotic movements, 212
Politics, as factor in immigration, 19, 77–80; expansion affects, 55; the immigrant in American, 82, 90–96, 211–212; Puritanism in, 99; as field for research, 209–213
Population, national origins of, 10–11; changes in European, 13–15, 192; movements of nineteenth-century, 18–23; mobility of American, 60–61; shifting of (1870's), 145; as factor in American development, 176–177
Populists, immigrant attitude toward, 90–91

Portuguese, on Cape Cod, 172–173
Powhaten, wrecked, 46
Princeton University, influence of, 120
Prohibition, Puritanism and, 100, 101, 111–112, 123, 127–128
Psenka, J. R., as author, 207 *n.*
Puritanism, interpretation of, 97–100; origin and development of, 100–104; practical aspect of, 104–105; ebbs, 106–107; coming of Irish causes revival of, 108–111; depression strengthens, 112; immigrant church promotes, 114–121; Catholic Church retards, 122; in the South, 123–125; slavery and, 125–126; prohibition and, 127–128

Quakers, prosecuted, 100, 124
Quebec, migration from, 170, 187; migration to, 180
Quota system, in 1920's, 10

Railroads, speed settlement, 75–76, 183–186, 197–198; as subject for research, 197–198
Raster, Hermann, as journalist, 208 *n.*
Red River country, developed, 185
Religion, immigrant conservatism in, 83, 91; Puritanism in, 98, 101, 112–123, 144; tolerance in, 107; as subject for research, 199. *See also* Churches
Republican party, the immigrant in, 92, 95; and Know Nothings, 136
Research topics: reasons for migration, 192–193; means of migrat-

ing, 193-195; immigration legislation, 195; process of distribution, 195-201; the immigrant in industry, 200-201; social life of the immigrant, 201-208; careers of journalists, 208 *n.*; immigrant societies, 209; the immigrant in politics, 209-213. *See also* Materials for research

Revival of 1858, 112

Revolutionary War, cause of, 54; radicalism and, 85

Rhode Island, Irish in, 155

Roebling, J. A., mentioned, 150

Roman Catholic Church, *see* Catholic Church

Sabbath, laws, 100, 104; desecrated, 106; Scandinavian observance of, 117; observance enforced, 120; observance in South, 124; observance in New Netherland, 124

Sadlier, Mary, as author, 207 *n.*

St. Louis, the immigrant in, 139; as immigrant distributing center, 196

Sanitation, on shipboard, 44-45, 47-48

Scandinavians, depart, 31; as pioneers, 73; condemn Haymarket rioters, 89; in politics, 90-92, 93; and Sabbath observance, 117-118; growth of nationalism among, 135-136; cultural development of, 136-137, 144; subject for research in congregations of, 199; as writers, 207 *n.*; agitate against migration, 212

Schurz, Carl, as refugee, 80

Scotch-Irish, in Pennsylvania, 87

Scots, in intellectual pursuits, 130; sent to New England, 154; Americanized, 155

Shays's Rebellion, and the Constitution, 85

Shields, James, as subject for study, 211 *n.*

Ships, described, 32-33; leave port, 33-34; roll call on, 34; stowaways on, 35; cooking on, 35-37; regulations on, 37, 40, 43-44; "clear the continent," 37-38; meet at sea, 39; industry on, 39, 41; amusements on, 41, 51; intellectual life on, 41-42; quarrels on, 42-43; self-government on, 43; health on, 44, 48; in storms, 45-46; wrecked, 46; delayed, 47-49; approach America, 49-51

Sinn Fein movement, 212 *n.*

Slavery, and Puritanism, 125-126

Slavs, in Lowell, Mass., 201

Smith, Adam, quoted, 13

Smith, Captain John, on discouragement of pioneers, 66

Social evolution, the immigrant influences, 11-13, 16, 22; diversity in, 24-25

Socialist party, the immigrant in, 95

Societies, commemorative, 26; for improving historical writing, 28; communistic, 86, 125; temperance, 105; Catholic clergy elected to, 107; secret, 111; Irish, 132; German singing, 139, 206; German dramatic, 139; agricultural, 168, 172; as subject for

research, 209; against immigration, 212
South, Puritanism in, 123-125; slavery in, 125-126; prohibition in, 126
South America, migration to, 20-21, 24
South Dakota, immigrant political influence in, 90-91
Speech, free, 213. *See also* Language
Statistics, nineteenth-century immigration, 4, 21; national-origins, 10-11; of immigrants in Civil War, 142; of Canadian migration, 176, 184; of immigration between 1815 and 1914, 191; in census of 1850, 196-197
Steerage, hardships, 3-4; described, 32-33; brawls, 42; cleanliness in, 44-45; occupants, 130
Strasbourg, migration via, 31
Strikes, the immigrant in, 88; English attitude toward, 169
Suffrage, *see* Woman suffrage
Sunday, *see* Sabbath
Swedes, as farmers, 151; migrate after Civil War, 168; in New England, 173
Syrians, in New England, 173

Temperance, society, 105; the Catholic Church and, 110, 123; enforced, 120; in the South, 126-127. *See also* Prohibition
Theater, *see* Drama
Timber trade, promotes immigration, 157-160, 194
Tobacco trade, aids immigration, 157, 194
Trade, in people, 5-7; in goods, 7-8; aids migration, 157-160; as a subject for research, 193-195; competition for, 194
Transportation, routes, 31, 37-38; difficulties, 129; as a subject for research, 196-198. *See also* Ships, Railroads
Turner, F. J., at Johns Hopkins, 56-57; formulates frontier theory, 57-58; disciples of, 58-59; dies, 59; influence of, 59
Turners, in America, 139

Ulster, migration from, 108, 125, 154
U. S. census, immigration data in (1850), 53-54, 196; on the frontier (1890), 58
University of Illinois, materials for research in, 28

Virginia, Puritanism in, 124, 125
Vlastos, S. J., as journalist, 208 *n.*

War of 1812, relation of expansion to, 54
Washington, migration to, 187
West Indies, migration to, 20
Westward movement, nature of, 53, 179-180; factors retarding, 59-60, 177-178; factors hastening, 60-65, 183-184; immigration influences, 65-76; first phase of, 178; as factor in Canadian-American relations, 180-181, 186-187. *See also* Frontier
White Star Line, routes, 6
Williamsburg, festivities in, 125
Winthrop, John, *Journal* of, 103

Wisconsin, the immigrant farmer in, 67; immigrant political influence in, 92–93; immigrant immorality in, 114 n.; Sunday observance in, 117; immigrant attitude toward draft law in, 142; Hamsun in, 149; migration from Canada to, 182, 187; popularity of, 196; Germans in, 199; materials for research in, 211

Witchcraft, outburst against, 105
Woman suffrage, immigrants oppose, 92
World War, influences migration, 17–18; hastens Americanization, 147; in foreign-language press, 208
Wyoming, suffrage in, 92

Yale University, influence of, 120

Revised Nov., 1963

harper ✥ torchbooks

HUMANITIES AND SOCIAL SCIENCES

American Studies

JOHN R. ALDEN: The American Revolution, 1775-1783. *Illus.* TB/3011

RAY A. BILLINGTON: The Far Western Frontier, 1830-1860. *Illus.* TB/3012

RANDOLPH S. BOURNE: The War and the Intellectuals: *A Collection of Essays, 1915-1919.* Edited with an Introduction by Carl Resek TB/3043

JOSEPH CHARLES: The Origins of the American Party System TB/1049

T. C. COCHRAN & WILLIAM MILLER: The Age of Enterprise: *A Social History of Industrial America* TB/1054

FOSTER RHEA DULLES: America's Rise to World Power, 1898-1954. *Illus.* TB/3021

W. A. DUNNING: Reconstruction, Political and Economic, 1865-1877 TB/1073

CLEMENT EATON: The Growth of Southern Civilization, 1790-1860. *Illus.* TB/3040

HAROLD U. FAULKNER: Politics, Reform and Expansion, 1890-1900. *Illus.* TB/3020

LOUIS FILLER: The Crusade against Slavery, 1830-1860. *Illus.* TB/3029

EDITORS OF FORTUNE: America in the Sixties: *the Economy and the Society. Two-color charts* TB/1015

LAWRENCE HENRY GIPSON: The Coming of the Revolution, 1763-1775. *Illus.* TB/3007

FRANCIS J. GRUND: Aristocracy in America: *Jacksonian Democracy* TB/1001

OSCAR HANDLIN, Editor: This Was America: *As Recorded by European Travelers to the Western Shore in the Eighteenth, Nineteenth, and Twentieth Centuries. Illus.* TB/1119

MARCUS LEE HANSEN: The Atlantic Migration: 1607-1860. Edited by Arthur M. Schlesinger; Introduction by Oscar Handlin TB/1052

MARCUS LEE HANSEN: The Immigrant in American History. Edited with a Foreword by Arthur Schlesinger, Sr. TB/1120

JOHN D. HICKS: Republican Ascendancy, 1921-1933.* *Illus.* TB/3041

JOHN HIGHAM, Ed.: The Reconstruction of American History TB/1068

ROBERT H. JACKSON: The Supreme Court in the American System of Government TB/1106

JOHN F. KENNEDY: A Nation of Immigrants. *Illus.* TB/1118

WILLIAM E. LEUCHTENBURG: Franklin D. Roosevelt and the New Deal, 1932-1940. *Illus.* TB/3025

LEONARD W. LEVY: Freedom of Speech and Press in Early American History: *Legacy of Suppression* TB/1109

ARTHUR S. LINK: Woodrow Wilson and the Progressive Era, 1910-1917. *Illus.* TB/3023

BERNARD MAYO: Myths and Men: *Patrick Henry, George Washington, Thomas Jefferson* TB/1108

JOHN C. MILLER: The Federalist Era, 1789-1801.*Illus.* TB/3027

PERRY MILLER & T. H. JOHNSON, Editors: The Puritans: *A Sourcebook of Their Writings*
Volume I TB/1093
Volume II TB/1094

GEORGE E. MOWRY: The Era of Theodore Roosevelt and the Birth of Modern America, 1900-1912.*Illus.* TB/3022

WALLACE NOTESTEIN: The English People on the Eve of Colonization, 1603-1630. *Illus.* TB/3006

RUSSEL BLAINE NYE: The Cultural Life of the New Nation, 1776-1801. *Illus.* TB/3026

GEORGE E. PROBST, Ed.: The Happy Republic: *A Reader in Tocqueville's America* TB/1060

FRANK THISTLETHWAITE: America and the Atlantic Community: *Anglo-American Aspects, 1790-1850* TB/1107

TWELVE SOUTHERNERS: I'll Take My Stand: *The South and the Agrarian Tradition. Introduction by Louis D. Rubin, Jr.; Biographical Essays by Virginia Rock* TB/1072

A. F. TYLER: Freedom's Ferment: *Phases of American Social History from the Revolution to the Outbreak of the Civil War. Illus.* TB/1074

GLYNDON G. VAN DEUSEN: The Jacksonian Era, 1828-1848. *Illus.* TB/3028

WALTER E. WEYL: The New Democracy: *An Essay on Certain Political and Economic Tendencies in the United States* TB/3042

LOUIS B. WRIGHT: The Cultural Life of the American Colonies, 1607-1763. *Illus.* TB/3005

LOUIS B. WRIGHT: Culture on the Moving Frontier TB/1053

Anthropology & Sociology

W. E. LE GROS CLARK: The Antecedents of Man: *An Introduction to the Evolution of the Primates. Illus.* TB/559

ST. CLAIR DRAKE & HORACE R. CAYTON: Black Metropolis: *A Study of Negro Life in a Northern City. Introduction by Everett C. Hughes. Tables, maps, charts and graphs* Volume I TB/1086
Volume II TB/1087

CORA DU BOIS: The People of Alor. *New Preface by the author. Illus.* Volume I TB/1042
Volume II TB/1043

L. S. B. LEAKEY: Adam's Ancestors: *The Evolution of Man and his Culture. Illus.* TB/1019

ROBERT H. LOWIE: Primitive Society. *Introduction by Fred Eggan* TB/1056

TALCOTT PARSONS & EDWARD A. SHILS, Editors: Toward a General Theory of Action: *Theoretical Foundations for the Social Sciences* TB/1083

SIR EDWARD TYLOR: The Origins of Culture. *Part I of "Primitive Culture." Introduction by Paul Radin* TB/33

SIR EDWARD TYLOR: Religion in Primitive Culture. *Part II of "Primitive Culture." Introduction by Paul Radin* TB/34

W. LLOYD WARNER: Social Class in America: *The Evaluation of Status* TB/1013

*The New American Nation Series, edited by Henry Steele Commager and Richard B. Morris.

I

Art and Art History

EMILE MÂLE: The Gothic Image: *Religious Art in France of the Thirteenth Century. 190 illus.* TB/44
ERWIN PANOFSKY: Studies in Iconology: *Humanistic Themes in the Art of the Renaissance. 180 illustrations* TB/1077
ALEXANDRE PIANKOFF: The Shrines of Tut-Ankh-Amon. *Edited by N. Rambova. 117 illus.* TB/2011
JEAN SEZNEC: The Survival of the Pagan Gods: *The Mythological Tradition and Its Place in Renaissance Humanism and Art. 108 illustrations* TB/2004
HEINRICH ZIMMER: Myths and Symbols in Indian Art and Civilization: *70 illustrations* TB/2005

Business, Economics & Economic History

REINHARD BENDIX: Work and Authority in Industry: *Ideologies of Management in the Course of Industrialization* TB/3035
THOMAS C. COCHRAN: The American Business System: *A Historical Perspective, 1900-1955* TB/1080
ROBERT DAHL & CHARLES E. LINDBLOM: Politics, Economics, and Welfare: *Planning and Politico-Economic Systems Resolved into Basic Social Processes* TB/3037
PETER F. DRUCKER: The New Society: *The Anatomy of Industrial Order* TB/1082
ROBERT L. HEILBRONER: The Great Ascent: *The Struggle for Economic Development* TB/3030
PAUL MANTOUX: The Industrial Revolution in the Eighteenth Century: *The Beginnings of the Modern Factory System in England* TB/1079
WILLIAM MILLER, Ed.: Men in Business: *Essays on the Historical Role of the Entrepreneur* TB/1081
PERRIN STRYKER: The Character of the Executive: *Eleven Studies in Managerial Qualities* TB/1041
PIERRE URI: Partnership for Progress. TB/3036

Contemporary Culture

JACQUES BARZUN: The House of Intellect TB/1051
JOHN U. NEF: Cultural Foundations of Industrial Civilization TB/1024
PAUL VALÉRY: The Outlook for Intelligence TB/2016

History: General

L. CARRINGTON GOODRICH: A Short History of the Chinese People. *Illus.* TB/3015
DAN N. JACOBS & HANS BAERWALD: Chinese Communism: *Selected Documents* TB/3031
BERNARD LEWIS: The Arabs in History TB/1029
SIR PERCY SYKES: A History of Exploration. *Introduction by John K. Wright* TB/1046

History: Ancient and Medieval

A. ANDREWES: The Greek Tyrants TB/1103
HELEN CAM: England before Elizabeth TB/1026
NORMAN COHN: The Pursuit of the Millennium: *Revolutionary Messianism in medieval and Reformation Europe and its bearing on modern totalitarian movements* TB/1037
G. G. COULTON: Medieval Village, Manor, and Monastery TB/1022
F. L. GANSHOF: Feudalism TB/1058

J. M. HUSSEY: The Byzantine World TB/1057
SAMUEL NOAH KRAMER: Sumerian Mythology TB/1055
FERDINAND LOT: The End of the Ancient World and the Beginnings of the Middle Ages. *Introduction by Glanville Downey* TB/1044
J. M. WALLACE-HADRILL: The Barbarian West: *The Early Middle Ages, A.D. 400-1000* TB/1061

History: Renaissance & Reformation

JACOB BURCKHARDT: The Civilization of the Renaissance in Italy. *Introduction by Benjamin Nelson and Charles Trinkaus. Illus.* Volume I TB/40
Volume II TB/41
ERNST CASSIRER: The Individual and the Cosmos in Renaissance Philosophy. *Translated with an Introduction by Mario Domandi* TB/1097
EDWARD P. CHEYNEY: The Dawn of a New Era, 1250-1453 †*Illus.* TB/3002
WALLACE K. FERGUSON, et al.: Facets of the Renaissance TB/1098
WALLACE K. FERGUSON, et al.: The Renaissance: *Six Essays. Illus.* TB/1084
MYRON P. GILMORE: The World of Humanism, 1453-1517. †*Illus.* TB/3003
JOHAN HUIZINGA: Erasmus and the Age of Reformation. *Illus.* TB/19
PAUL O. KRISTELLER: Renaissance Thought: *The Classic, Scholastic, and Humanist Strains* TB/1048
NICCOLO MACHIAVELLI: History of Florence and of the Affairs of Italy: *from the earliest times to the death of Lorenzo the Magnificent. Introduction by Felix Gilbert* TB/1027
ALFRED VON MARTIN: Sociology of the Renaissance. *Introduction by W. K. Ferguson* TB/1099
J. E. NEALE: The Age of Catherine de Medici TB/1085
ERWIN PANOFSKY: Studies in Iconology: *Humanistic Themes in the Art of the Renaissance. 180 illustrations* TB/1077
J. H. PARRY: The Establishment of the European Hegemony: 1415-1715: *Trade and Exploration in the Age of the Renaissance* TB/1045
HENRI PIRENNE: Early Democracies in the Low Countries: *Urban Society and Political Conflict in the Middle Ages and the Renaissance. Introduction by John H. Mundy* TB/1110
FERDINAND SCHEVILL: The Medici. *Illus.* TB/1010
FERDINAND SCHEVILL: Medieval and Renaissance Florence. *Illus.* Volume I: *Medieval Florence* TB/1090
Volume II: *The Coming of Humanism and the Age of the Medici* TB/1091
G. M. TREVELYAN: England in the Age of Wycliffe, 1368-1520 TB/1112
VESPASIANO: Renaissance Princes, Popes, and Prelates: *The Vespasiano Memoirs: Lives of Illustrious Men of the XVth Century. Introduction by Myron P. Gilmore. Illus.* TB/1111

History: Modern European

FREDERICK B. ARTZ: Reaction and Revolution, 1815-1832. †*Illus.* TB/3034
MAX BELOFF: The Age of Absolutism, 1660-1815 TB/1062
ROBERT C. BINKLEY: Realism and Nationalism, 1852-1871. †*Illus.* TB/3038
CRANE BRINTON: A Decade of Revolution, 1789-1799. †*Illus.* TB/3018

†*The Rise of Modern Europe Series*, edited by **William L. Langer**.

J. BRONOWSKI & BRUCE MAZLISH: The Western Intellectual Tradition: *From Leonardo to Hegel* TB/3001
GEOFFREY BRUUN: Europe and the French Imperium, 1799-1814. †*Illus.* TB/3033
WALTER L. DORN: Competition for Empire, 1740-1763. †*Illus.* TB/3032
CARL J. FRIEDRICH: The Age of the Baroque, 1610-1660. †*Illus.* TB/3004
LEO GERSHOY: From Despotism to Revolution, 1763-1789. †*Illus.* TB/3017
ALBERT GOODWIN: The French Revolution TB/1064
CARLTON J. H. HAYES: A Generation of Materialism, 1871-1900. †*Illus.* TB/3039
J. H. HEXTER: Reappraisals in History: *New Views on History and Society in Early Modern Europe* TB/1100
A. R. HUMPHREYS: The Augustan World: *Society, Thought, and Letters in Eighteenth Century England* TB/1105
DAN N. JACOBS, Ed.: The New Communist Manifesto and Related Documents TB/1078
HANS KOHN, Ed.: The Mind of Modern Russia: *Historical and Political Thought of Russia's Great Age* TB/1065
SIR LEWIS NAMIER: Vanished Supremacies: *Essays on European History, 1812-1918* TB/1088
JOHN U. NEF: Western Civilization Since the Renaissance: *Peace, War, Industry, and the Arts* TB/1113
FREDERICK L. NUSSBAUM: The Triumph of Science and Reason, 1660-1685. †*Illus.* TB/3009
RAYMOND W. POSTGATE, Ed.: Revolution from 1789 to 1906: *Selected Documents* TB/1063
PENFIELD ROBERTS: The Quest for Security, 1715-1740. †*Illus.* TB/3016
PRISCILLA ROBERTSON: Revolutions of 1848: *A Social History* TB/1025
N. N. SUKHANOV: The Russian Revolution, 1917: *Eyewitness Account.* Edited by Joel Carmichael
Volume I TB/1066
Volume II TB/1067
JOHN B. WOLF: The Emergence of the Great Powers, 1685-1715. †*Illus.* TB/3010
JOHN B. WOLF: France: 1814-1919: *The Rise of a Liberal-Democratic Society* TB/3019

Intellectual History

HERSCHEL BAKER: The Image of Man: *A Study of the Idea of Human Dignity in Classical Antiquity, the Middle Ages, and the Renaissance* TB/1047
J. BRONOWSKI & BRUCE MAZLISH: The Western Intellectual Tradition: *From Leonardo to Hegel* TB/3001
NORMAN COHN: The Pursuit of the Millennium: *Revolutionary Messianism in medieval and Reformation Europe and its bearing on modern totalitarian movements* TB/1037
ARTHUR O. LOVEJOY: The Great Chain of Being: *A Study of the History of an Idea* TB/1009
ROBERT PAYNE: Hubris: *A Study of Pride.* Foreword by Sir Herbert Read TB/1031
BRUNO SNELL: The Discovery of the Mind: *The Greek Origins of European Thought* TB/1018

Literature, Poetry, The Novel & Criticism

JAMES BAIRD: Ishmael: *The Art of Melville in the Contexts of International Primitivism* TB/1023
JACQUES BARZUN: The House of Intellect TB/1051

W. J. BATE: From Classic to Romantic: *Premises of Taste in Eighteenth Century England* TB/1036
RACHEL BESPALOFF: On the Iliad TB/2006
R. P. BLACKMUR, et al.: Lectures in Criticism. Introduction by Huntington Cairns TB/2003
ABRAHAM CAHAN: The Rise of David Levinsky: *a novel.* Introduction by John Higham TB/1028
ERNST R. CURTIUS: European Literature and the Latin Middle Ages TB/2015
GEORGE ELIOT: Daniel Deronda: *a novel.* Introduction by F. R. Leavis TB/1039
ETIENNE GILSON: Dante and Philosophy TB/1089
ALFRED HARBAGE: As They Liked It: *A Study of Shakespeare's Moral Artistry* TB/1035
STANLEY R. HOPPER, Ed.: Spiritual Problems in Contemporary Literature TB/21
A. R. HUMPHREYS: The Augustan World: *Society, Thought, and Letters in Eighteenth Century England* TB/1105
ALDOUS HUXLEY: Antic Hay & The Gioconda Smile. TB/3503
ALDOUS HUXLEY: Brave New World & Brave New World Revisited. Introduction by C. P. Snow TB/3501
ALDOUS HUXLEY: Point Counter Point. Introduction by C. P. Snow TB/3502
HENRY JAMES: The Princess Casamassima: *a novel.* Introduction by Clinton F. Oliver TB/1005
HENRY JAMES: Roderick Hudson: *a novel.* Introduction by Leon Edel TB/1016
HENRY JAMES: The Tragic Muse: *a novel.* Introduction by Leon Edel TB/1017
ARNOLD KETTLE: An Introduction to the English Novel. Volume I: *Defoe to George Eliot* TB/1011
Volume II: *Henry James to the Present* TB/1012
JOHN STUART MILL: On Bentham and Coleridge. Introduction by F. R. Leavis TB/1070
PERRY MILLER & T. H. JOHNSON, Editors: The Puritans: *A Sourcebook of Their Writings*
Volume I TB/1093
Volume II TB/1094
KENNETH B. MURDOCK: Literature and Theology in Colonial New England TB/99
SAMUEL PEPYS: The Diary of Samuel Pepys. Edited by O. F. Morshead. Illustrations by Ernest Shepard TB/1007
ST.-JOHN PERSE: Seamarks TB/2002
O. E. RÖLVAAG: Giants in the Earth. Introduction by Einar Haugen TB/3504
GEORGE SANTAYANA: Interpretations of Poetry and Religion TB/9
C. P. SNOW: Time of Hope: *a novel* TB/1040
DOROTHY VAN GHENT: The English Novel: *Form and Function* TB/1050
E. B. WHITE: One Man's Meat. Introduction by Walter Blair TB/3505
MORTON DAUWEN ZABEL, Editor: Literary Opinion in America
Volume I TB/3013
Volume II TB/3014

Myth, Symbol & Folklore

JOSEPH CAMPBELL, Editor: Pagan and Christian Mysteries TB/2013
MIRCEA ELIADE: Cosmos and History: *The Myth of the Eternal Return* TB/2050
C. G. JUNG & C. KERÉNYI: Essays on a Science of Mythology: *The Myths of the Divine Child and the Divine Maiden* TB/2014

ERWIN PANOFSKY: Studies in Iconology: *Humanistic Themes in the Art of the Renaissance*. 180 illustrations TB/1077
JEAN SEZNEC: The Survival of the Pagan Gods: *The Mythological Tradition and its Place in Renaissance Humanism and Art*. 108 illustrations TB/2004
HEINRICH ZIMMER: Myths and Symbols in Indian Art and Civilization. *70 illustrations* TB/2005

Philosophy

HENRI BERGSON: Time and Free Will: *An Essay on the Immediate Data of Consciousness* TB/1021
H. J. BLACKHAM: Six Existentialist Thinkers: *Kierkegaard, Nietzsche, Jaspers, Marcel, Heidegger, Sartre* TB/1002
ERNST CASSIRER: Rousseau, Kant and Goethe. *Introduction by Peter Gay* TB/1092
FREDERICK COPLESTON: Medieval Philosophy TB/76
F. M. CORNFORD: From Religion to Philosophy: *A Study in the Origins of Western Speculation* TB/20
WILFRID DESAN: The Tragic Finale: *An Essay on the Philosophy of Jean-Paul Sartre* TB/1030
PAUL FRIEDLANDER: Plato: *An Introduction* TB/2017
ETIENNE GILSON: Dante and Philosophy TB/1089
WILLIAM CHASE GREENE: Moira: *Fate, Good, and Evil in Greek Thought* TB/1104
W. K. C. GUTHRIE: The Greek Philosophers: *From Thales to Aristotle* TB/1008
F. H. HEINEMANN: Existentialism and the Modern Predicament TB/28
IMMANUEL KANT: The Doctrine of Virtue, *being Part II of The Metaphysic of Morals. Translated with Notes and Introduction by Mary J. Gregor. Foreword by H. J. Paton* TB/110
IMMANUEL KANT: Lectures on Ethics. *Introduction by Lewis W. Beck* TB/105
WILLARD VAN ORMAN QUINE: From a Logical Point of View: *Logico-Philosophical Essays* TB/566
BERTRAND RUSSELL et al.: The Philosophy of Bertrand Russell. *Edited by Paul Arthur Schilpp*
Volume I TB/1095
Volume II TB/1096
L. S. STEBBING: A Modern Introduction to Logic TB/538
ALFRED NORTH WHITEHEAD: Process and Reality: *An Essay in Cosmology* TB/1033
WILHELM WINDELBAND: A History of Philosophy I: *Greek, Roman, Medieval* TB/38
WILHELM WINDELBAND: A History of Philosophy II: *Renaissance, Enlightenment, Modern* TB/39

Philosophy of History

NICOLAS BERDYAEV: The Beginning and the End TB/14
NICOLAS BERDYAEV: The Destiny of Man TB/61
WILHELM DILTHEY: Pattern and Meaning in History: *Thoughts on History and Society. Edited with an Introduction by H. P. Rickman* TB/1075
JOSE ORTEGA Y GASSET: The Modern Theme. *Introduction by Jose Ferrater Mora* TB/1038
H. J. PATON & RAYMOND KLIBANSKY, Eds.: Philosophy and History TB/1115
W. H. WALSH: Philosophy of History: *An Introduction* TB/1020

Political Science & Government

JEREMY BENTHAM: The Handbook of Political Fallacies: *Introduction by Crane Brinton* TB/1069
KENNETH E. BOULDING: Conflict and Defense: *A General Theory* TB/3024
CRANE BRINTON: English Political Thought in the Nineteenth Century TB/1071
ROBERT DAHL & CHARLES E. LINDBLOM: Politics, Economics, and Welfare: *Planning and Politico-Economic Systems Resolved into Basic Social Processes* TB/3037
JOHN NEVILLE FIGGIS: Political Thought from Gerson to Grotius: 1414-1625: *Seven Studies. Introduction by Garrett Mattingly* TB/1032
F. L. GANSHOF: Feudalism TB/1058
G. P. GOOCH: English Democratic Ideas in the Seventeenth Century TB/1006
ROBERT H. JACKSON: The Supreme Court in the American System of Government TB/1106
KINGSLEY MARTIN: French Liberal Thought in the Eighteenth Century: *A Study of Political Ideas from Bayle to Condorcet* TB/1114
J. P. MAYER: Alexis de Tocqueville: *A Biographical Study in Political Science* TB/1014
JOHN STUART MILL: On Bentham and Coleridge. *Introduction by F. R. Leavis* TB/1070
JOHN B. MORRALL: Political Thought in Medieval Times TB/1076
KARL R. POPPER: The Open Society and Its Enemies
Volume I: *The Spell of Plato* TB/1101
Volume II: *The High Tide of Prophecy: Hegel, Marx, and the Aftermath* TB/1102
JOSEPH A. SCHUMPETER: Capitalism, Socialism and Democracy TB/3008

Psychology

ANTON T. BOISEN: The Exploration of the Inner World: *A Study of Mental Disorder and Religious Experience* TB/87
WALTER BROMBERG: The Mind of Man: *A History of Psychotherapy and Psychoanalysis* TB/1003
SIGMUND FREUD: On Creativity and the Unconscious: *Papers on the Psychology of Art, Literature, Love, Religion. Intro. by Benjamin Nelson* TB/45
C. JUDSON HERRICK: The Evolution of Human Nature TB/545
ALDOUS HUXLEY: The Devils of Loudun: *A Study in the Psychology of Power Politics and Mystical Religion in the France of Cardinal Richelieu* TB/60
WILLIAM JAMES: Psychology: *The Briefer Course. Edited with an Intro. by Gordon Allport* TB/1034
C. G. JUNG: Psychological Reflections. *Edited by Jolande Jacobi* TB/2001
C. G. JUNG: Symbols of Transformation: *An Analysis of the Prelude to a Case of Schizophrenia*
Volume I TB/2009
Volume II TB/2010
C. G. JUNG & C. KERÉNYI: Essays on a Science of Mythology: *The Myths of the Divine Child and the Divine Maiden* TB/2014
ERICH NEUMANN: Amor and Psyche: *The Psychic Development of the Feminine* TB/2012
ERICH NEUMANN: The Origins and History of Consciousness Volume I *Illus.* TB/2007
Volume II TB/2008

RELIGION

Ancient & Classical

J. H. BREASTED: Development of Religion and Thought in Ancient Egypt. *Introduction by John A. Wilson* TB/57
HENRI FRANKFORT: Ancient Egyptian Religion: *An Interpretation* TB/77
G. RACHEL LEVY: Religious Conceptions of the Stone Age *and their Influence upon European Thought. Illus. Introduction by Henri Frankfort* TB/106
MARTIN P. NILSSON: Greek Folk Religion. *Foreword by Arthur Darby Nock* TB/78
ALEXANDRE PIANKOFF: The Shrines of Tut-Ankh-Amon. *Edited by N. Rambova. 117 illus.* TB/2011
H. J. ROSE: Religion in Greece and Rome TB/55

Biblical Thought & Literature

W. F. ALBRIGHT: The Biblical Period from Abraham to Ezra TB/102
C. K. BARRETT, Ed.: The New Testament Background: *Selected Documents* TB/86
C. H. DODD: The Authority of the Bible TB/43
M. S. ENSLIN: Christian Beginnings TB/5
M. S. ENSLIN: The Literature of the Christian Movement TB/6
H. E. FOSDICK: A Guide to Understanding the Bible TB/2
H. H. ROWLEY: The Growth of the Old Testament TB/107
D. WINTON THOMAS, Ed.: Documents from Old Testament Times TB/85

Christianity: Origins & Early Development

EDWARD GIBBON: The Triumph of Christendom in the Roman Empire *(Chaps. XV-XX of "Decline and Fall," J. B. Bury edition). Illus.* TB/46
MAURICE GOGUEL: Jesus and the Origins of Christianity. *Introduction by C. Leslie Mitton*
Volume I: *Prolegomena to the Life of Jesus* TB/65
Volume II: *The Life of Jesus* TB/66
EDGAR J. GOODSPEED: A Life of Jesus TB/1
ADOLF HARNACK: The Mission and Expansion of Christianity *in the First Three Centuries. Introduction by Jaroslav Pelikan* TB/92
R. K. HARRISON: The Dead Sea Scrolls: *An Introduction* TB/84
EDWIN HATCH: The Influence of Greek Ideas on Christianity. *Introduction and Bibliography by Frederick C. Grant* TB/18
ARTHUR DARBY NOCK: Early Gentile Christianity and Its Hellenistic Background TB/111
JOHANNES WEISS: Earliest Christianity: *A History of the Period A.D. 30-150. Introduction and Bibilography by Frederick C. Grant* Volume I TB/53
Volume II TB/54

Christianity: The Middle Ages and After

G. P. FEDOTOV: The Russian Religious Mind: *Kievan Christianity, the tenth to the thirteenth centuries* TB/70
ETIENNE GILSON: Dante and Philosophy TB/1089
WILLIAM HALLER: The Rise of Puritanism TB/22
JOHAN HUIZINGA: Erasmus and the Age of Reformation. *Illus.* TB/19

A. C. McGIFFERT: Protestant Thought Before Kant. *Preface by Jaroslav Pelikan* TB/93
KENNETH B. MURDOCK: Literature and Theology in Colonial New England TB/99
H. O. TAYLOR: The Emergence of Christian Culture in the West: *The Classical Heritage of the Middle Ages. Intro. and biblio. by Kenneth M. Setton* TB/48

Judaic Thought & Literature

MARTIN BUBER: Eclipse of God: *Studies in the Relation Between Religion and Philosophy* TB/12
MARTIN BUBER: Moses: *The Revelation and the Covenant* TB/27
MARTIN BUBER: Pointing the Way. *Introduction by Maurice S. Friedman* TB/103
MARTIN BUBER: The Prophetic Faith TB/73
MARTIN BUBER: Two Types of Faith: *the interpenetration of Judaism and Christianity* TB/75
MAURICE S. FRIEDMAN: Martin Buber: *The Life of Dialogue* TB/64
FLAVIUS JOSEPHUS: The Great Roman-Jewish War, *with* The Life of Josephus. *Introduction by William R. Farmer* TB/74
T. J. MEEK: Hebrew Origins TB/69

Oriental Religions: Far Eastern, Near Eastern

TOR ANDRAE: Mohammed: *The Man and His Faith* TB/62
EDWARD CONZE: Buddhism: *Its Essence and Development. Foreword by Arthur Waley* TB/58
EDWARD CONZE, et al., Editors: Buddhist Texts Through the Ages TB/113
H. G. CREEL: Confucius and the Chinese Way TB/63

Philosophy of Religion

RUDOLF BULTMANN: History and Eschatology: *The Presence of Eternity* TB/91
RUDOLF BULTMANN AND FIVE CRITICS: Kerygma and Myth: *A Theological Debate* TB/80
RUDOLF BULTMANN and KARL KUNDSIN: Form Criticism: *Two Essays on New Testament Research. Translated by Frederick C. Grant* TB/96
MIRCEA ELIADE: The Sacred and the Profane TB/81
LUDWIG FEUERBACH: The Essence of Christianity. *Introduction by Karl Barth. Foreword by H. Richard Niebuhr* TB/11
ADOLF HARNACK: What is Christianity? *Introduction by Rudolf Bultmann* TB/17
FRIEDRICH HEGEL: On Christianity: *Early Theological Writings. Edited by Richard Kroner and T. M. Knox* TB/79
KARL HEIM: Christian Faith and Natural Science TB/16
IMMANUEL KANT: Religion Within the Limits of Reason Alone. *Introduction by Theodore M. Greene and John Silber* TB/67
PIERRE TEILHARD DE CHARDIN: The Phenomenon of Man TB/83

Religion, Culture & Society

C. C. GILLISPIE: Genesis and Geology: *The Decades before Darwin* TB/51
H. RICHARD NIEBUHR: Christ and Culture TB/3
H. RICHARD NIEBUHR: The Kingdom of God in America TB/49
ERNST TROELTSCH: The Social Teaching of the Christian Churches. *Introduction by H. Richard Niebuhr* Volume I TB/71
Volume II TB/72

Religious Thinkers & Traditions

AUGUSTINE: An Augustine Synthesis. *Edited by Erich Przywara* TB/35
KARL BARTH: Church Dogmatics: *A Selection: Introduction by H. Gollwitzer; Edited by G. W. Bromiley* TB/95
KARL BARTH: Dogmatics in Outline TB/56
KARL BARTH: The Word of God and the Word of Man TB/13
THOMAS CORBISHLEY: Roman Catholicism TB/112
ADOLF DEISSMANN: Paul: *A Study in Social and Religious History* TB/15
JOHANNES ECKHART: Meister Eckhart: *A Modern Translation by R. B. Blakney* TB/8
WINTHROP HUDSON: The Great Tradition of the American Churches TB/98
SOREN KIERKEGAARD: Edifying Discourses. *Edited with an Introduction by Paul Holmer* TB/32
SOREN KIERKEGAARD: The Journals of Kierkegaard. *Edited with an Intro. by Alexander Dru* TB/52
SOREN KIERKEGAARD: The Point of View for My Work as an Author: *A Report to History. Preface by Benjamin Nelson* TB/88
SOREN KIERKEGAARD: The Present Age. *Translated and edited by Alexander Dru. Introduction by Walter Kaufmann* TB/94
SOREN KIERKEGAARD: Purity of Heart. *Translated by Douglas Steere* TB/4
WALTER LOWRIE: Kierkegaard: *A Life*
  Volume I TB/89
  Volume II TB/90
GABRIEL MARCEL: Homo Viator: *Introduction to a Metaphysic of Hope* TB/97
PERRY MILLER & T. H. JOHNSON, Editors: The Puritans: *A Sourcebook of Their Writings*
  Volume I TB/1093
  Volume II TB/1094
A. D. NOCK: St. Paul TB/104
PAUL PFUETZE: Self, Society, Existence: *Human Nature and Dialogue in the Thought of George Herbert Mead and Martin Buber* TB/1059
F. SCHLEIERMACHER: The Christian Faith. *Introduction by Richard R. Niebuhr* Volume I TB/108
  Volume II TB/109
F. SCHLEIERMACHER: On Religion: *Speeches to Its Cultured Despisers. Intro. by Rudolf Otto* TB/36
PAUL TILLICH: Dynamics of Faith TB/42
EVELYN UNDERHILL: Worship TB/10
G. VAN DER LEEUW: Religion in Essence and Manifestation: *A Study in Phenomenology. Appendices by Hans H. Penner* Volume I TB/100
  Volume II TB/101

NATURAL SCIENCES AND MATHEMATICS

Biological Sciences

CHARLOTTE AUERBACH: The Science of Genetics TB/568
A. BELLAIRS: Reptiles: *Life History, Evolution, and Structure. Illus.* TB/520
LUDWIG VON BERTALANFFY: Modern Theories of Development: *An Introduction to Theoretical Biology* TB/554
LUDWIG VON BERTALANFFY: Problems of Life: *An Evaluation of Modern Biological and Scientific Thought* TB/521

HAROLD F. BLUM: Time's Arrow and Evolution TB/555
A. J. CAIN: Animal Species and their Evolution. *Illus.* TB/519
WALTER B. CANNON: Bodily Changes in Pain, Hunger, Fear and Rage. *Illus.* TB/562
W. E. LE GROS CLARK: The Antecedents of Man: *An Introduction to the Evolution of the Primates. Illus.* TB/559
W. H. DOWDESWELL: Animal Ecology. *Illus.* TB/543
W. H. DOWDESWELL: The Mechanism of Evolution. *Illus.* TB/527
R. W. GERARD: Unresting Cells. *Illus.* TB/541
DAVID LACK: Darwin's Finches. *Illus.* TB/544
J. E. MORTON: Molluscs: *An Introduction to their Form and Functions. Illus.* TB/529
O. W. RICHARDS: The Social Insects. *Illus.* TB/542
P. M. SHEPPARD: Natural Selection and Heredity. *Illus.* TB/528
EDMUND W. SINNOTT: Cell and Psyche: *The Biology of Purpose* TB/546
C. H. WADDINGTON: How Animals Develop. *Illus.* TB/553

Chemistry

A. FINDLAY: Chemistry in the Service of Man. *Illus.* TB/524
J. R. PARTINGTON: A Short History of Chemistry. *Illus.* TB/522
J. READ: A Direct Entry to Organic Chemistry. *Illus.* TB/523
J. READ: Through Alchemy to Chemistry. *Illus.* TB/561

Geography

R. E. COKER: This Great and Wide Sea: *An Introduction to Oceanography and Marine Biology. Illus.* TB/551
F. K. HARE: The Restless Atmosphere TB/560

History of Science

W. DAMPIER, Ed.: Readings in the Literature of Science. *Illus.* TB/512
ALEXANDRE KOYRÉ: From the Closed World to the Infinite Universe: *Copernicus, Kepler, Galileo, Newton, etc.* TB/31
A. G. VAN MELSEN: From Atomos to Atom: *A History of the Concept Atom* TB/517
O. NEUGEBAUER: The Exact Sciences in Antiquity TB/552
H. T. PLEDGE: Science Since 1500: *A Short History of Mathematics, Physics, Chemistry and Biology. Illus.* TB/506
GEORGE SARTON: Ancient Science and Modern Civilization TB/501
HANS THIRRING: Energy for Man: *From Windmills to Nuclear Power* TB/556
WILLIAM LAW WHYTE: Essay on Atomism: *From Democritus to 1960* TB/565
A. WOLF: A History of Science, Technology and Philosophy in the 16th and 17th Centuries. *Illus.*
  Volume I TB/508
  Volume II TB/509
A. WOLF: A History of Science, Technology, and Philosophy in the Eighteenth Century. *Illus.*
  Volume I TB/539
  Volume II TB/540

Mathematics

H. DAVENPORT: The Higher Arithmetic: *An Introduction to the Theory of Numbers* TB/526
H. G. FORDER: Geometry: *An Introduction* TB/548
GOTTLOB FREGE: The Foundations of Arithmetic: *A Logico-Mathematical Enquiry into the Concept of Number* TB/534
S. KÖRNER: The Philosophy of Mathematics: *An Introduction* TB/547
D. E. LITTLEWOOD: Skeleton Key of Mathematics: *A Simple Account of Complex Algebraic Problems* TB/525
GEORGE E. OWEN: Fundamentals of Scientific Mathematics TB/569
WILLARD VAN ORMAN QUINE: Mathematical Logic TB/558
O. G. SUTTON: Mathematics in Action. *Foreword by James R. Newman. Illus.* TB/518
FREDERICK WAISMANN: Introduction to Mathematical Thinking. *Foreword by Karl Menger* TB/511

Philosophy of Science

R. B. BRAITHWAITE: Scientific Explanation TB/515
J. BRONOWSKI: Science and Human Values. *Illus.* TB/505
ALBERT EINSTEIN: Philosopher-Scientist. *Edited by Paul A. Schilpp* Volume I TB/502
Volume II TB/503
WERNER HEISENBERG: Physics and Philosophy: *The Revolution in Modern Science. Introduction by F. S. C. Northrop* TB/549
JOHN MAYNARD KEYNES: A Treatise on Probability. *Introduction by N. R. Hanson* TB/557
STEPHEN TOULMIN: Foresight and Understanding: *An Enquiry into the Aims of Science. Foreword by Jacques Barzun* TB/564
STEPHEN TOULMIN: The Philosophy of Science: *An Introduction* TB/513
W. H. WATSON: On Understanding Physics. *Introduction by Ernest Nagel* TB/507
G. J. WHITROW: The Natural Philosophy of Time TB/563

Physics and Cosmology

DAVID BOHM: Causality and Chance in Modern Physics. *Foreword by Louis de Broglie* TB/536
P. W. BRIDGMAN: The Nature of Thermodynamics TB/537
LOUIS DE BROGLIE: Physics and Microphysics. *Foreword by Albert Einstein* TB/514
T. G. COWLING: Molecules in Motion: *An Introduction to the Kinetic Theory of Gases. Illus.* TB/516
A. C. CROMBIE, Ed.: Turning Point in Physics TB/535
C. V. DURELL: Readable Relativity. *Foreword by Freeman J. Dyson* TB/530
ARTHUR EDDINGTON: Space, Time and Gravitation: *An outline of the General Relativity Theory* TB/510
GEORGE GAMOW: Biography of Physics TB/567
MAX JAMMER: Concepts of Force: *A Study in the Foundation of Dynamics* TB/550
MAX JAMMER: Concepts of Space: *The History of Theories of Space in Physics. Foreword by Albert Einstein* TB/533
EDMUND WHITTAKER: History of the Theories of Aether and Electricity
Volume I: *The Classical Theories* TB/531
Volume II: *The Modern Theories* TB/532
G. J. WHITROW: The Structure and Evolution of the Universe: *An Introduction to Cosmology. Illus.* TB/504

Code to Torchbook Libraries:

TB/1+ : The Cloister Library
TB/501+ : The Science Library
TB/1001+ : The Academy Library
TB/2001+ : The Bollingen Library
TB/3001+ : The University Library

A LETTER TO THE READER

Overseas, there is considerable belief that we are a country of extreme conservatism and that we cannot accommodate to social change.

Books about America in the hands of readers abroad can help change those ideas.

The U. S. Information Agency cannot, by itself, meet the vast need for books about the United States.

You can help.

Harper Torchbooks provides three packets of books on American history, economics, sociology, literature and politics to help meet the need.

To send a packet of Torchbooks [*] overseas, all you need do is send your check for $7 (which includes cost of shipping) to Harper & Row. The U. S. Information Agency will distribute the books to libraries, schools, and other centers all over the world.

I ask every American to support this program, part of a worldwide BOOKS USA campaign.

I ask you to share in the opportunity to help tell others about America.

signature

EDWARD R. MURROW
Director,
U. S. Information Agency

[*retailing at $10.85 to $12.00]

PACKET I: *Twentieth Century America*
   Dulles/America's Rise to World Power, 1898-1954
   Cochran/The American Business System, 1900-1955
   Zabel, Editor/Literary Opinion in America (two volumes)
   Drucker/The New Society: *The Anatomy of Industrial Order*
   Fortune Editors/America in the Sixties: *The Economy and the Society*

PACKET II: *American History*
   Billington/The Far Western Frontier, 1830-1860
   Mowry/The Era of Theodore Roosevelt and the
      Birth of Modern America, 1900-1912
   Faulkner/Politics, Reform, and Expansion, 1890-1900
   Cochran & Miller/The Age of Enterprise: *A Social History of Industrial America*
   Tyler/Freedom's Ferment: *American Social History from the Revolution to the Civil War*

PACKET III: *American History*
   Hansen/The Atlantic Migration, 1607-1860
   Degler/Out of Our Past: *The Forces that Shaped Modern America*
   Probst, Editor/The Happy Republic: *A Reader in Tocqueville's America*
   Alden/The American Revolution, 1775-1783
   Wright/The Cultural Life of the American Colonies, 1607-1763

Your gift will be acknowledged directly to you by the overseas recipient. Simply fill out the coupon, detach and mail with your check or money order.

HARPER & ROW, PUBLISHERS · BOOKS USA DEPT.
49 East 33rd Street, New York 16, N. Y.

Packet I ☐   Packet II ☐   Packet III ☐

Please send the BOOKS USA library packet(s) indicated above, in my name, to the area checked below. Enclosed is my remittance in the amount of _____ for _____ packet(s) at $7.00 each.

_____ Africa   _____ Latin America

_____ Far East   _____ Near East

Name_____

Address_____

NOTE: This offer expires December 31, 1966.